A DIARY OF AN EIGHTEENTH-CENTURY GARDEN

BY THE HAND OF

Dion Clayton Calthrop

WITH DECORATIONS
BY

Eleanor Fortescue Brickdale

"What is this life,
   if full of care,
We have no time to stand and stare.
No time to stand beneath the boughs
And stare as long as sheep or cows.
No time to see when woods we pass
Where squirrels hide their nuts in grass"

———

A DIARY OF AN EIGHTEENTH-CENTURY GARDEN

17 68

SICUT UMBRA

You must, if you please, keep this picture in your mind. There is a fire in Mr. Anderson's study owing to a hint of frost in the air, just enough frost to cause the logs to burn blue flame now and again. He is a man of about fifty with a face of classic mould, a Roman face not uncommon in England. His coat is wide-skirted and his wig is a bob major, ruffles of fine lace adorn his wrists, and his neckcloth is from Ypres. By him on the hearthrug lies his pointer, Don, his nose on his paws, his mind in wet turnip fields where is a covey of partridges.

On a large table lie two books of manuscript neatly written in the Italian hand: the one closed is Mr. Anderson's Bee Book, in which he has just noted " By this time your Bees sit; keep them close Night and

Morning." The open book is his Garden Book, in which he keeps notes of his parterre and garden together with garden lore. He notes such things as the origin of the name of the Jerusalem artichoke, which is Italian and a corruption of gie a sole, to turn to the sun, and alongside he notes that the heliotrope does likewise, but is so called from the Greek : helio tropos.

If we glance over his shoulder, we shall see that he has but recently planted a Judas tree with the note " On this Tree it is said that Judas did hang himself. Told me by Colonel Thornton Bridges." Let us notice, also, that he has written down the recipe for making damson, medlar and crab apple cheese with a memorandum " To ask Mrs. Madbury the correct way to make Cowslip Wine."

" I favour the old names," he writes, " and I am pleased my gardener, James Spalding, should use them. Though in other ways he is a silent man he talks to children, animals and flowers. Yesternoon he told me five names for the Pansy to which I did add a sixth, Pensé for a thought, yet he would have none of it. Herb Trinity he calls them, and Three Faces under a Hood, and Love in Idleness, Stepmother, and Hearts

Ease. A peasant will make his Poetry out of the Earth how ever hard times may be. It is from him my housekeeper has the knowledge to knit stockings of three colours in wool learnt from a pedlar out of Scotland, who gave him also the country name of Venice Mallow, which is ' Goodnight at noon.' A pretty conceit and true ! "

Mr. Anderson's spelling is not all it might be, and he likes a flourish to his capital letters, but he is a true countryman and can find his way by the stars and knows the use of simples, and grows all manner of wild things in his garden in a wilderness he keeps. Here he will have celandine and shepherd's purse, sauce alone and rocket, which he calls dames violet; and he grows balsam, which is touch-me-not; and here also are penny cress and traveller's joy, which is old man's beard or lady's bower.

He hesitates whether to put down " The Cure for a Cough " in his Bee Book or among his Garden Notes. Finally he decides for the Garden Notes :

Told me by Mrs. Cocker (aet. 81). To ease a trouble-some cough.

Syrup of Horehound	..	..	..	1 oz.
„ „ Poppies	..	..	..	.. 1 oz.
„ „ Squills	..	..	..	.. 1 oz.
Clarified Honey	..	..	..	.. 1 oz.

Two teaspoonfuls to be taken on going to roost, and rising, in a teacupful of warm water, or during the day if the cough be troublesome.

Among Mr. Anderson's notes are many such entries as these : cures for toothache, a mixture called " Live Long," " To make Durable Ink," " To Pot Mussels," etc. Here is one for the preparation of " Lavendar Water " :

One quart of the purest rectified spirits of wine.
Two oz. of the best oil of Lavendar. (The English extract.)
Two oz. of Bergamot.
Four grains of Musk, if liked.
Half an oz. of the essence of Ambergin.

To be mixed all together and kept well corked in a warm place and repeatedly to be shaken up. It will be fit for use in a month, but if kept a year is much better. (Note. Excellent good. J. R. A.)

We may make sure that all the good man's linen lies in lavendar, and that his bowls are full of pot-pourri.

Outside in his garden room, which knows the scent of tobacco and iced punch well enough, we can see him take a survey of his red-walled property with its well-ordered walks all box edged, the kitchen herbs out of sight in a garden of their own, the bees humming as they work, the rooks cawing in the elms, the sound of shears as they clip the yew hedge. It is permissible here for Mr. Anderson to divest himself of his wig and wear but a silk scarf to hide his shaven head.

Mr. Anderson, as one can see from his Garden Diary, has little use for the town. " There is not," he writes, " a pair of Red Heels to be seen within ten miles of London. We have no place for them here be they on the shoes of Rakes or Dappers, Pretty Fellows or Politicians. And I wonder if I should care to see Phœbus self in Petticoats parading on the lawn. Your Beauty plucks at flowers so carelessly even to cull herself a Nosegay that she nip off the head of a rose take one sniff at it & throw it away. As for Sir Pertinax Hatton, the fellow when he paid me a visit poked about my flowers with his cane as if they grew of themselves without tending quoting meanwhile some rubbishy verses on the Dullness of the Country. ' Stap me ! ' the puppy said. ' I protest you are all mould here.' (Note : I gave him some French Claret which had gone a little sour telling him it was of the finest which he declared to be so. And it was good enough for any Jack-a-napes even though his father be My Lord Judge and what-not.")

I read further and find great rest and refreshment in the record of this country gentleman's peaceful and orderly life, and I quote here another note of his :

Came yesterday a great lumbering fellow out of the Fens in the neighbourhood of Whaplode, a regular Gaby in a smocked frock. I was reading Juvenal when Polly, the maid, told me one Samuel wished to speak to me. Anon came this raw countryman twisting at his smock and grinning like a dead sheep. It seemed he claimed a right of coarse fishing in certain Drains as we call them and brought for his payment of fee a hare (which he swore he had found) some golden plover and an old bone box, very dirty, which he told me he had fished up.

I told him he was no better than a Poacher, at which he burst forth into lamentations as said he had been proclaimed as such, but if fish would come to his hook and hares die by his feet and plover flew in at his window what was a man to do. I rated him soundly and told him he was a bad case and that the law was made to see to such persons as he, after which I bade the maids to give him bacon and ale having called them by whistling which is a habit I have.

(Note : To cook golden plover. Captain James recipe.)

(Note : To keep flies out of your rooms in Summer place on the Sills pots of Sweet scented Musk which they utterly abhor so Miss D. L. told me, as also to place India Muslin over your outdoor meat safe against Blue-bottles.)

Mixed with these notes are Thoughts on Religion, all of the kindly charitable character which breathes through this country gentleman and flavours all his meditations. There are bird notes also, as

April 8th.—The first swallow doth appear to grace the sky, anon will come plenty and as pretty a sight as winter dimmed eyes could wish for. Sea Gulls come far inland betokening foul weather at sea. They come into my garden and will eat a mess of toast keeping away the lesser birds all but the Starlings who thieve pieces from them.

April 12th.—I have a thrush who works for me in my garden breaking snails upon a stone afterwards eating them and then giving praise to God from the topmost bough of a tree.

May 2nd.—Come a sweet little maid to see me with a basket of eggs from my friend Lady Sarah Thorpe. Gave her a kiss and some comfits. The pretty Innocence of children is a Delight to the Heart.

I will leave these notes now and continue later with such cullings as may interest my readers.

My friend does not merely dream his life away among his books or under his favourite tree, but endeavours to keep company with all manner of men whose conversation is not purely frivolous. He has a good sense of humour as any man and can tell a story against himself with relish.

Among his notes he places anything curious that he hears or that comes under his immediate notice. For example, I find that he is at pains to discover the origin of the names given to flowers both wild and cultivated. " Some names," he writes, " seem to spring from no recognizable source yet they obtain up & down the countryside where a man will speak of the plant ' Good King Henry ' not knowing it to be called also ' English Mercury.' Which King Henry can he mean ? "

Of " Monk's Rhubarb " (Rumea Patientia) he can see clearly that it is a medicinal plant and comes under the order of Simples (which he often spells " ffimples ") as were collected and cultivated in those days when a knowledge of herbs was a necessary precaution in life. With these so-called pot herbs comes also herb patience.

In his day there were many wise women who brewed concoctions against all manner of evils and also as love potions. In the notes especially on herbs one finds names which at once suggest fragrance of both history and poetry.

" Sweet Marjoram," he writes, " what fragrant thoughts arise at the sound of such names as these. ' Herb Teucer,' ' Germander,' ' Wound Wort,' ' Wild Thyme ' and ' Pennyroyal ' and ' Meadow Sage.' In the twilight of Botany such names arose and bloomed through the night of the Dark Ages until the day broke, but in those mists a country Poet sang of simple things near to the Earth as Adam."

Did (this for a fancy) the herb twopence gain its name from the first financier and did that careful man give it its Latin name in order to hide the secret of his

wealth from the ever greedy : " Lysimachia num-
mularia " ?

Our country poet finds names in this green island
awaiting him, to nameless plants and flowers he gives
names by a godfatherdom of his own, and as I read
Mr. Anderson I see how justly he sets down not only
the learned names but the little names, the first love
names.   But, mark you, he has method too.

March 1st.—Now the Windes come fiercely bind
your weakest Plants against they become prostrate.
Now is the Time to sow Pinks and Sweet Williams
and Carnations.   Acquaint your Greenhouse and Conservatory gradually with the air by Day but trust not
the Night.   Beware the sudden darking of the Sun
and also the Frosts and sharp Winds.   If the season
be dry water your Anemony roots well once or twice
a week.   Be careful also that the East Winds do not
prejudice your choicest plants, as Tulips and Jacynths
but shelter them with mats.

In April Mr. Anderson's advice is :

that you do now sow Hyssop, Basile, Thyme and

Scurvey Grass. Entertain such Exotic plants as you may possess in fresh hot beds with the Art to preserve them and foster them during this Season.

It is now the time of Laycock, White Thorn, Musk, Florence Iris, Lady's Smock and White Violets.

This is the Time to distil Plants for Waters.

Set your Bees at Liberty but expect swarms.

Note : Some say Gilly-flowers should be planted by Full Moon, but such sayings creep in from one knows not where. Though they be Heathen still the Heathen kept flowers and knew of many strange Devices.

For May Mr. Anderson notes that " Snails should be gathered after Rain. Set also tempting baits against the ravages of Insects. Now are flowering both white and blue Campanulas, as is also the Deptford Pink and Homer's Moly with many other flowers too numerous to set down."

He has his Duke, Flanders and heart cherries, black, white and red, also the Luke-ward and Naples cherries, and at this time he has strawberries, corinths and melons.

In June he notes that " Aviary birds grow sick of their feathers so that he makes Emulsions for them of Melon and Cucumber seeds, and gives them Groundsel, and Chickweed &, if he has some, of the Pome-Granade seeds."

So placid a man as Mr. Anderson has a temper besides for the follies of the people who will not provide for themselves. " There are people in this world," he writes, " who have no thought for the Winter. They never dry a herb or pickle onions or the seeds of the Nasturtium, nor will they keep a Tub of Brine and lay by such pieces of Pig as the Ears, Tail, etc., which would serve them for the winter months. So I must ask my neighbours for old Cloakes & cast away shoes & many other things as old Linen, Medicines & Stale Bread. Mr. Endover doth give me wood for the cutting but Lord these fanglish people as soon cut themselves as wood and a man will as soon drink Gin and other Strong Waters and Smoak his pipe as tend his piece of garden."

Then follows without due sequence of idea a note. " The Bill of a Property Man to a Theatre. (Lord how strange to see how effects are come by)."

	£	s.	d.
For Hire of Six Case of Pistols ..		4	o
A Drum for Mrs. Bignall in the Pilgrim		4	4
A Truss of Straw for the Madmen ..			8
Pomatum and Vermilion to Grease the Face of the Stuttering Cook ..			8
For Boarding a Setting Dog Two Day to follow Mr. Johnson in Epsom-Wells			6
For Blood in Macbeth			3
Raisins and Almonds for a Witches Banquet			8

In July he is at the perpetual war gardeners wage against insects. He straightens the entrance to his bee hives and sets about killing drones. Then he sets glasses of beer mingled with honey to entice wasps and flyes, and he hangs these bottles near his nectarines and other tempting fruits. " Else many times they invade your best Fruit." He seeks diligently for snails under the leaves of his mural trees and makes a decoction of tobacco refuse, brine, potash and water with which to water his gravel walks so as to destroy worms and weeds.

In August he makes his cider and perry, keeping his choice apples, such as the Ladies' Longing, Sheepssnout and Cushion apples for the table. At Bartholomew-tide Mr. Anderson removes and lays his perennial greens, his jasmines and oleanders and translates them to moist and shaded ground.

With all these garden cares and delights Mr. Anderson is happy, but naturally he is not free from the ills the flesh is heir to. There are boys who break in and steal his choice fruit, there is swine fever in the neighbourhood, his favourite horse goes lame and himself suffers from a twinge of " that plaguey thing, the gout." He notes that " cats will eat & destroy your Marum Syriac if they can come at it." And that robbing insects and wasps must continually be destroyed.

" Last week," he wrotes, " comes Sir Abel Rawley out of the Town and brings me news of the Great World, but O how stale and unprofitable it is and sounds so in my quiet & peace. That Brocade Sword Knots be not worn, that Bat Pigeon is the only wigmaker of elegance ; that Lady —— hath an affair with a low ill bred fellow : and how some madman preaches that a Plague will fall on the Earth by Christmas and utterly destroy all who go to Playhouse & Taverns, these things vex the ear and are vain & small in the country."

Now the good man is at seeing the autumn leaves and swept and gathered together to make good mould ; he is taking care that his carnations do not get too wet and so rot. He is preparing against wind and frost, rolling his grass walks and finishing his last weeding.

Now Mr. Anderson prepares for the end of the year, cutting logs for his hearth, trenching his ground and digging in manure. He covers up his bees and turns the fruit in the store room lest it taint. His fruit trees are pruned and nailed to the walls and all in the garden is in order. The fountain pipes are covered with straw against the frost and the conservatory doors are looked to to see that they shut out the cold air.

Here is the last entry in this diary :

Dec. 31*st.*—I do thank God for all this Goodness and Mercy to me in this year, guarding me from loss

and from illness of any grave order. I thank Him for the abundant yield of Fruit and Flowers which are a solace to the mind causing man to live simple and in great content.

All flesh is grass. J. R. A.

September.—Comes Betty, one of my maids, a good lass, but ever over hurried, who tells me a gentleman is come to ask for me.

When she has recovered her breath I ask her what manner of gentleman this may be, to which she replies, " A very fine gentleman, sir, as fine as ever I saw."

This proves to be my old friend Cornelious Brand, a curious fellow, who spends his days wandering.

I bid the maids to set a room in order at once, telling them Mr. Brand is to have the South room and every attention to his order as it were myself.

(Mem. : Silent men are always the greatest talkers.)

It is nigh on three years since I clapt eyes on Cornelious and here he comes and passes the time of day with me as it were we met but yesterday, and that with my garden in full autumn beauty, but he looks round and does say, but, " Great content," and drinks his bottle of claret sniffing at the bouquet and taking a pinch of snuff now and again to appease his nostrils.

After dinner, at which, please God, he was a hearty trencherman, eating stewed eels, the best part of a duck and twice of good mutton, he opens his mouth after half a bottle of port and tells me he is lately out of France and Italy, having walked like any mendicant.

" Lord, Jack," he says, speaking pat, " I must give a guinea to your cook, and buss her, if she be comely, for that duck, for I am sick of kickshaws. I want no more of Italian oil or French vinegar for a long time and I trow, Jack, there are more eggs and less meat in France than in all the world. But, Lord, the mountains, man, I am grown to love mountains more than women, both change ever, but the mountains do not talk, both have infinite variety, but one is due to Nature and the other to fashion." (Note : To quote same in company.)

This friend hath a manner of speaking so vigorous that it puts life into a man to hear him, but he do fill my garden so full that it seems the very flowers pale beside him, yet we have many friendly silences withal. He loves big spaces, great trees, large dogs and healthy

children and can charm a shy bird to come to him.
(Mem. : In reading my chapter in The Book to-night
I am minded of David and his great ways. Methinks
Cornelious might put a man into the forefront of the
battle. On second thoughts—" Judge not and ye shall
not be judged.")

(Mem. : To ask Mrs. Heath how to make a Cornish
Pasty.)

I had but to put a question here and there to keep
the flow of his talk in a straight course, for he would
speak of wars and flowers in one breath, but in all I
did get the wind of his conversation to blow from the
south.

" Lord, man ! " he said to me, " Had I not spoke
French as do the natives I might not be alive, but I do
that and also took my brushes and colours with me
and that is a visé with the French, for they conceive
an artist to be a legitimate madman. In the South
the people who live in the mountains are a simple,
God-fearing people and they harboured me well.

" Lord, man ! The spring ! (Note : I will leave
out his divers strange oaths.) And trouts do abound
so that any man may have a good meal for the asking

and the peasants say God put them in the waters for Friday's eating, which is a pretty thought in these Papists.

" In the pastures through which run these streams, and by the roadside, grow countless flowers, making your heart rejoice in their beauty. Of gentians, not a few, and the mealy primulas standing dainty with their feet in streams, and daffodils and the narcissi so plentiful that men scythe them : the white lily they call Saint Bruno, marvellous beautiful, together with Daphne and the Bears Grape Hyacynth. In such guise the feet of the hills are clothed so that a man may feel not so lonely in face of the great mountains covered with snow and ice, carrying man's thoughts to solitude. You have peace here, Jack, but what a peace is theirs !

" The meat grows at your elbow, the fish at your feet, corn sings in the valley where are coneys and a multitude chickens.

" In Italy, too, they have flowers, but not so richly set, and they eat a good dish of paste of flour with Tomatoes and cheese as good as a man can care for, but the wines are not so good, except one cares for the wine they call Chianti, very palatable ! "

Talking and drinking we were till dawn and I none too tired yet, feeling I had travelled far in those hours and could feel the prick of the sun on my eyeballs. So when Cornelious had retired (I helping him to bed, he being merry and singing), I made myself a brew of lime flower water and betook myself into my garden, there to enjoy the solace of early morning and to hear the thrushes sing matins and to smell the flowers come fresh out of their sleep.

December.—Here is snow, very seasonable and plentitude of berries on the holly, which I like muchly to see, though some say it means a hard winter, which is cruel for the poor.

Last night for the first time this year I did have my warming pan in my bed and a fire of wood from the old elm which was blown down in the storm. It is sad, but it did provide me, not only with firewood, but with a good rook pie many birds being shot by my groom, for which I did upbraid him ; yet the pie was good (Mr. Smalley's method to cook a rook pie). Mr. Smalley, a sweet reasonable man and very delicate in all manner of food and drink and says a snipe and a woodcock must but fly through the kitchen and a

Teal hung eight days. He told me also the manner in which false marrow may be made : to take fat of salted beef and cut it up very fine and serve with a toast of bread. Excellent good.

A sharper frost that men say has not been known in sixty years, the river frozen solid, and cattle found dead in fields and birds to the very doors of houses for water. In my garden abundance of starlings, tits, thrushes and blackbirds, which is cousin to a thrush, but not so sweet in song to my thinking, and yesternoon two reed warblers and a redstart come to eat of my bread and grain. These little servants of God move me mightily and I do thank God Who made provision for the recesses of our nature so we may rejoice in little things and look in awe at the magnitude of His creation.

To-day comes an old man for years a worker in my water meadows, ten years crippled with the Rheumaticks and now upright and would wish to work again. He took but an old wives' tale that he must sting himself with bees and did so and now all his pains are gone and I did marvel, but there it was.

Thank God for the Cordials I caused to be made

last year, so now I have abundance of Elderberry, Cowslip and Ginger Cordials, also Plum, Crab Apple and Damson Cheese. My cook hath also preserved red and white currants in sugar, which make elegant dishes to grace my table.

Seventeenth.—Hear to-day of a matter now laughable, but was like at one time to be nigh tragical. One Coles, a plover netter, essaying to pass over the ice by Hoplode Drove, did fall in and was near to drowning, being full of strong ale, but his dog, seeing the affaire did turn his posterior to his master and by barking showed him how he might use his tail for a rope, so he was saved and the dog none the worse.

(Mem. : To cure a whitlow, an onion very hot bound tight about the place.)

Comes my bailiff to request me to see what he hath fatting for Christmas, and a good sight it was, though in a manner pitiful for the birds and pigs. I have twelve geese, of which I give ten away, as usual, also four pigs, very fat, seven ducks and a few capons.

As God, through my fathers, has given me plenty, it is well to give in plenty, so I bade my cook to make twenty cakes, very rich, for the poor of this parish and to kill three of the pigs to make a feast with a cask of ale. (To give kindling also ?)

In my fruit house now a great abundance of apples and many winter pears, together with herbs now well dried. My frames do still yield me a salad and I have good store of potatoes.

Mem. : Mrs. Hornblower hath told me to fry some potatoes in bacon fat and keep them and to warm them when need be for a side dish : also to keep peas in a bottle and preserve them green.

My garden now under a mantle of snow and my bee skeps with old cloth about them, so my bees shall not perish.

Later.—The church choir to visit me with carols of that good King who did look out on the feast of Stephen and many others. Mighty pretty to see and to hear, with lanthorns gleaming on the snow and the cobbler playing on his fiddle.

The year is nigh gone and my garden is trenched ; my fruit is now turned in the fruit house, the apples in good order and none bruised or sweating. Of Pears my baking and roasting pears, especially French Wardens, do excel, being covered with straw against the frost. The Bergamot, very good to eat now and full of juice. Even the great frost and snow have not burst my Fountain pipes and only one of my water barrells hath burst its hoops.

Much merriment of Mummers who made the old play for me before the house and then asked in and ale given hot with sops of toast, the Dragon and St. George taking ale together most friendly and singing an old catch older than their father's fathers. Then a bowl of good punch (Sir Andrew Orvell's recipe). We drank to Absent Friends and they did make much of me in a speech spoke by an old man, Giles Orton, very prettily put and with much mirth, so I left him and went to wind my clocks.

April 1st.—All Fools' Day, so called from the foolish custom to take people in by stating such things as " your wig is awry," when it is not so. But in truth April hath a more comely meaning, being from the Latin, *aperire*, to open, when in truth do buds and plants open to the first warmth which maketh the heart of man to rejoice.

This year come the martins and swallows very early, and soon my ears shall be gladdened by the sound of Master Cuckoo, and with him comes also Cuckoo Pint in the hedgerows.

Now will come quickly the Marsh Marybuds and the new leaf on the elm, and anon I shall hear the snipe piping and the Greenfinch also.

Now reading " Love's Labour's Lost," by W. Shakespeare, and mark finding therein :

> When daisies pied, and violets blue,
> And lady-smocks all silver-white,
> And cuckoo-birds of yellow hue,
> Do paint the meadows with delight.

April 12th.—They say a proverb is the wisdom of

many and the wit of one, but how true this may be I know not, but that to " ne'er cast a clout before May be out " is a wise saw, for this year, Lord knows, I am tricked already by three warm days and now back again into a shirt of knitted woollen make (Scots).

April 19*th.*—Up early and to church, where a good few to early service. Myself going fasting and so home in vexation until I had broken my fast.

Later through my orchard and to my fishing, there being many trout in the stream although sorely poached. I waited there for a long time in pleasant meditation before even setting up my rod, the day being warm and a South wind gently stirring, trouts leaping in the pool and all Nature a harmony.

April is above all Months for loveliness, with the orchard trees beginning to bloom and the birds scattering their songs from branch to branch. *Mem. :* to cook brown trout the angler's way. Split open and clean your fish and wrap it in sheets of paper, greasing the one next to the fish with plenty of good butter. Set this parcel in a draught and set a light to it. It will burn slow at first, but after the fire will come at the butter and flare your fish. Excellent good to eat.

28

On a day like this (writ in my study after dinner) a man may well rejoice if he have even little money and no illness. In a moment Winter is forgotten and Spring casts her magic. She has mantled her bosom with the blue Hyacinth and made her raiment glad with the golden Cowslip. The Snowdrop, Fair Maid of February my maids call her, is gone, and all the earth is pricked by little flowers. W. Shakespeare speaks of " the uncertain glory of an April day." This is indeed true, for the skies weep without warning and then comes the Sun to kiss the tears away.

I cease now to set out food for the birds, as in Winter, there being now worms, snails and insects, but I do not wish this year for bullfinches to make merry with my fruit-buds; they strip trees if over many settle in my garden. A pretty fellow, but a glutton.

Lord Herbert of Cherbury wrote in his poems :

> " The watery ground that late did mourn
> Was strewed with flowers for the return
> Of the wished bridegroom to the earth.
> The well-accorded birds did sing
> And warbling murmurs of a brook
> And varied notes of leaves that shook
> An harmony of pasts did bind."

My lord wrote so over an hundred years gone by and April hath not changed, so I am minded to say, rather to ask if Man himself changes except upon his outer fashions. My grandfather snuffed his Violet Strasburg, or Best Brazil, and I snuff Dutch Rappe ; periwigs are not out yet, and in the town still hangs a sign over a Tobacco shop of his day, with three men seated by a barrel and under is painted :

> " We three are engaged in one cause,
> I snuffs, I smoaks, and I chaws."

My grandfather would speak of a maid with " watchet " eyes, meaning thereby that her eyes were blue, and he would speak of a little bundle of sticks as a " trousseau," which it is, the word meaning a little bundle.

My grandmother kept a little book in which she wrote prayers and meditations, pieces of poetry, country sayings and notes of her possessions of which I have some yet, notably a gold repeating watch made by a Frenchman, a Bible bound in Shagreen, a silver Posnet to butter Eggs, a Cheese Toaster, and an Adam and Eve without Fig-leaves in Bugle Work upon Canvas, curiously wrought by her own hand.

I must beg of you now to allow me again to draw a picture of this sterling Englishman consulting his gardener John Spalding, totting up the accounts of his estate, picking up local news, watching the fishing-boats coming up the broad river from the Wash, friend to everybody but the snob, the ill-mannered, the bore and the cruel person. You may see him reading his favourite Classics, or out of Gervase Markham's "Country House-Wife's Garden," in the "Paradisus in Sole" by John Parkinson, and thus warming his five wits by the aid of his reading candles, horn-rimmed spectacles and a jorum of brandy; a contented man.

One thing, local as far as he knew, delighted him, and that was the custom of placing weathercocks on trees on the days farmers feasted their servants.

"To-day," he writes, "came on a sight which is ever pleasing to me, and that is seeing the gay innocence of weathercocks on the trees, newly placed there. It be a strange merry thing to see the Twelve Apostles in wood turning hither and thither in the wind, which counts not Saint Peter or Saint Barnabas favourite, but takes all alike and at its fancy. I had one gave to me by Roger Quiltam to show bird, beast and fish blowing through an Ark, with Mister Noë waving his arms this and that way. A quaint device (one shilling and two pennies).

" All men are children, and so God loves them, and if so be these toys keep away the Devil, who shall be better pleased than Man born of Woman whose Heel is on the Serpent's Head ?

" I bade this rough fellow R. Quiltam to me to give him his monies and he told me his father and his father's father did make this same weathercock for their masters, and that he would contrive a Jonah to be swallowed and vomited by the Whale when the West Wind blew, so I gave him 1 shilling again to his pains.

" I hope that men will always be good craftsmen such as we have about us, namely George Winter, who doth build the best staircase and rails in one hundred miles ; the Puller family, weavers ; Noel Bushkin, a truly great carver, whose mantel at Hoodam is the admired of all beholders ; Roger Blake, the Sign Painter, a drunken fellow but a marvel with his brush, as witness The Green Man, The Coach and Horses, and many others ; Molly Ponder do make as

good a moleskin waistcoat as any London snip, and can kill a pig as quick as Rob: Ornish the butcher.

" To London next week against my will, but I must see to some affairs there, notably the £342 owed me by sale of some houses."

Reading in a book of Verse entitled " Love of Fame, the Universal Passion," which my bookseller hath sent me. Herein the author speaks shewdly of the religion of the fashionable young woman, and I do hold his wit not to be misplaced.

" From Atheists far, they steadfastly believe
    God is, and is Almighty—to forgive.
    His other excellence they'll not dispute;
    But *Mercy*, sure, is His chief attribute.
    Shall pleasure of a short duration chain
    A lady's soul in everlasting pain?
    Will the great Author us poor worms destroy,
    For now and then a sip of transient joy?
    No, He's for ever in a smiling mood,
    He's like themselves; or how could He be good?
    And they blaspheme who blacker schemes suppose—
    Devoutly, thus, Jehovah they depose,
    The pure ! the just ! and set up in His stead
    A Deity that's perfectly well-bred."

34

This author, I find, do set down deep thoughts but with a light hand, as it were to gild his satiric pill to suit the Fashionable World; to write as one who whispers prayers in an Assembly Room.

> " The love of gaming is the worst of ills,
>   With ceaseless storms the blackened soul it fills,
>   Inveighs at heav'n, neglects the ties of blood,
>   Destroys the power and will of doing good,
>   Kills health, pawns honour, plunges in disgrace,
>   And, what is still more dreadful—spoils your face."

Again the author do speak of over good living and do touch me in a point, as I am not amiss to good fare yet I do not carry the taste to his extreme.

> " The genius of a dish some justly taste,
>   And eat their way to fame : with anxious thought
> The salmon is refused, the turbot bought.
> Impatient Art rebukes the sun's delay,
> And bids December yield the fruits of May.
> Their various cases in one great point combine
> The business of their life, that is—to dine."

But he doth correct me too for my Garden, but I can see the fellow is no gardener himself, albeit he do mention the name of a beautiful Tulip, Paul Diack :

> " We smile at Florists, we despise their joy,
>   And think their hearts enamoured of a toy ;

35

> But are those wiser whom we most admire,
> Survey with envy, and pursue with fire?
> What's he who sighs for fame, or wealth, or power?
> Another Florio doating on a flower,
> A short-lived flower, and which has often sprung
> From sordid acts, as Florio's out of dung."

I will set this down also :

> " Courts can give nothing to the wise or good
> But scorn of Pomp, or love of Solitude,
> High stations tumult, but not bliss, create ;
> None thinks the Great unhappy but the Great."

    .   .   .   .   .   .

In my study, with a vile chill come from wet and
cold come from shooting of snipe in the boggy meadows,
so much at home by my fire and taking a book here
and there not read for a long time. So I read the Odes
of Horace again and do find him vastly opposed to
Garlick, which he do claim to be more baneful than
Hemlock, yet is Garlick the plant of the gods and is a
good thing used sparsely to flavour a dish. But I do
find this poet admires drink and women even above
the simple pleasures of the country though he praise
Vine and Olive. In reading him he seems a lewd,
clever fellow, holding wine to be the solace of every

evil, and, smeared with Persian scents, will have the Lyre played to tease away his vapours.

'Tis said that Latin is a Gentleman's tongue, and we have many elegant writers in that language. Jonson, Crashaw, Milton, Marvel, Addison, Gray and others. So in reading Ode 1, I was forced to translate for myself, smiling not a little at my rusty imperfections :

" The huntsman, unmindful of his tender spouse,
remains in the cold air, whether a hart is held in view
by his faithful hounds, or a Marsian boar has broken
the circling toils."

For here had I been (but with no tender spouse) catching a chill from going after small birds with my fowling-piece.

(Note : Multitude of frogs croaking tonight which they call here the Lincolnshire bagpipes and is a sign of rain.)

My cook, good soul, did bring me to drink last night a Possett of mulled wine with spices and I know not what, so I took this and fell into a deep sleep. After a time I seemed to wake and to be in a garden of exquisite beauty where flowers of all seasons bloomed together, birds sang and a fountain of water made music with the bees. Here were little cabinets of yew to rest within, and pomegranates growing by cut hedges of holly, and on the brick walls all manner of fruits growing in profusion. As I did wander through I saw alleys of grass leading to bowling greens with Tulips set orderly and in every colour, with bees working in them making their muffled song. Bird answered bird, and none was harsh, and a wind blew soft as if over a warm and spiced land. (The Possett ?)

Anon I did come to Grotts, and by them great basins of water where stone nymphs bathed, and by these citrons and oranges and fig-trees. And here, where aviaries of artificial birds caused to sing by a mechanism of water flowing through great and small pipes cunningly hid, and Myrils and Cypresse casting their reposeful shadows on walls painted with Allegorical Scenes as Venus rising from the Sea, etc.; very pretty.

Here I never spied a gardener but yet saw how well all was kept and the hedges and arbours trimmed and no leaf on the paths, yet did I see sprigs set to catch woodcock on the trees.

Saw also, in my dreams, many devices of wind to

toss up balls of copper from a stone pavement, and to make groanings in rocky caverns where water trickled over ferns.

This do come of much reading and the examination of pictures for I saw poplar trees and the lily Arum, and date-palms and roses like to scarlet fires, and the Italian Mimosa the like of which do only grow to prospering in our houses of glass.

Once the daughter of my friend Mrs. N. K. did conjure me out of myself with her singing so that I was remarked as a dreamer, and I said that dreams are glorious cloaks given to us to hide the tatters of our daily life, and this I did say almost then in a dream.

(I would give more for ten minutes with a man who cannot be sure but that he has seen an Angel, than I would give for a week with a man who laughs at all he cannot lay his fingers on.)

Friday.—Comes a present from my old friend Jesse Newlands, a man very resourceful in all manner of learning. He hath sent me a book writ by himself and notably bound, and having for title " The Golden Rose, by a Gentleman of Leisure."

The title he hath taken from that Rose of Gold which the Pope of Rome doth bless on the Fourth Sunday in Lent, and is sent to great persons. The Pope do dip the Rose in balsam, sprinkles it with Holy Water, and incenses it. It was carried to Henry VIII by Pope Julius II, and by Pope Leo X and also to other great persons.

Many things of roses are set down in this book, as that Sir John Mandeville do say the red rose be sprung from the extinguished brands heaped about a virgin Martyr called Zillah. This same maid was tormented by a drunken fellow called Hamrel, and as she did refuse all attention of his, he gave out she was possessed of a devil, and so she was put to the stake, but God did avert the flames and there grew instead a tree of red and white roses about her.

The Rose do also stand Emblem for England and besides for the reconnaissance of the Richmonds, whereby they might be recognised on the field of battle and in journeyings. He do say, also, that the red rose was the badge of Edmund Plantagenet, second son to Henry III, this Edmund being the first Duke of Lancaster, and the white rose is the badge of the House of York. The white rose now is the sign of the followers of The Pretender, for they do meet, as men say, " *sub rosa.*"

The Papists do place a rose over confessionals as a sign of secrecy and silence, and so was placed in the ceiling of Haddon Hall that the guests might know what was spoken in the great Hall of Banquets was in the strictest confidence.

So we come at Harpocrates, the God of Silence, who was given a Rose by Cupid to bribe him that Venus' amours might not be betrayed.

He doth remark also how the Early Saints had the Rose for symbol, as St. Dorothea, St. Casilda, St. Elizabeth of Portugal, St. Rose of Lima, and St. Rose of Viterbo.

My learned author doth go from the Rose Noble, a coin of Edward III, worth in his day 8s. 6d. but to-day I do not know what ; to the Rose window in churches, the nozzles of watering-cans, to the wind Rose which is a device set in the belly of a wind instrument such as a lute, dulcimer and harpsichord, until he do come to those " roses worth a family " which the Elizabethan wore on his shoes and covered with Rose diamonds after the Dutch fashion of cutting. At last he bids us make merry at The Rose Coffee House in Bow Street, where Dryden held himself master of the wits.

(Mem. : to tell my cook to gather the hips of the Dog Rose (Rosa Canina) to make a conserve as the book directs.)

After setting the book down I was much struck by the History one flower can make, how it can make Wars, and be a conceit of Love and Silence, of Music, Money, Religion and a Sweetmeat.

Of every flower there must be much tradition, and

of the Lily it is said that it sprang from the tears of
the repentant Eve as she came out of the Garden of
Paradise, and so was given to the Virgin Mary to be
her symbol, and St. Joseph do hold a lily also to show
Paradise come again on earth.

Some do say that to labour is to pray, but I do say
" to labour is to pray to cease labouring." The sweets
of toil are these hours in which a man may lay down
his task and straighten his back, and regard his accom-
plishment. A man is bowed in all his work, the
merchant at his accounts, the lawyer at his documents,
the author at his desk. A painter will best stand to
his work, a singer also, and one who would address the
people for their betterment, but as a whole man stoops
at his task.

To-day I took a spade to dig round the roots of some
fruit-trees the better to air them and put in mulch to
feed them, and when I rose and set my back straight,
and wiped the sweat from my brow with the back of
my hand, I could feel as men felt who first cried,
" Corn in Egypt."

The sun and rain and wind do labour to bless the
earth with fruitfulness, and the moon, men say, turns

the tide, and the stars in their steadfast places do aid the mariner, being God's night-lights to those at sea so that a ship may come at her port in safety through God's guidance. It is said that such a man be born under a lucky star, but it do mean that if a man will but steer a true course under God's guidance he shall arrive truly at the Port of Heaven.

At his leisure a man may collect the image and wonder of the day, and, taking from it his gross appetites, he may gain peace of mind, rebuke evil fancies and set his soul at rest.

All night long the trees and flowers in my garden are growing above and under the soil. In the morning I have often rejoiced to see a bud hath opened in a rose-bush, or little leaves come out upon the trees. My heart doth sing to see the first catkin or pussy-willow; the first primrose or violet; the first violet, the first lambs, and the first tender break in the sky.

London.—But writ at home.—I vowed, an I returned alive, to set down some account of my visit to London, where I went over a matter of business. But Lord, what a place ! My head yet in a commotion by it and memory of little account. The noise terrible and one must shout in the streets to be heard.

Was took by M. Rawlinson to many Coffee Houses to see the life there. In some they smoake Tobacco, game and drink all day. At the Cocoa Tree, where we went first, the talk is mostly of Politics, of the Errors of Government, of Bribes and the buying and selling of places. A man here boasts he could get me to be a Lord for £300, which I was told was true, but I would liefer be plain Esquire and keep my honesty (and my £300).

We have corrupt men in the Country but they do not boast about it openly, but here a merchant will tell how he has brought people swiftly to poverty and the company will laugh at his crafty ways.

At Hamlin's four clergymen very drunk and pow-
dered with snuff making great argument on Free Will
and the like.   My swine I swear are cleaner company.

Batson's more precise and full of merchants who
talked of Pepper, Spices and Indigo.   M. Rawlinson
told me Child and the Chapter is the place clergy go to
who seek preferment and there they talk of Glebes,
Advowsons, Rectories and Lectureships.

The great men keep to their own Houses.   Addison,
Steele, Swift and Pope go most to Button's ; Hogarth
and Fielding to the Bedford, but M. Rawlinson told
me Wills has been for a long time the House for men
of letters, and spoke to seeing Dryden there and many
others.   At the Chapter House do the Booksellers meet.

Next day in talk with Mister Arne he told me a man
might now live on £200, and save £30, having a wife,
four children, a maid, a man, and a boy to run errands.
Bread for all costing four shillings, coal for the year
£8 10.   (Mem. : my coal is £14.)   Physic £2.   Entertainment, £4.

My own window tax is 9 shillings, an iniquitous
tax and should be put down, but they say will be
increased, to take the duty off tea.

At four of the morning one may be quiet except for the noise of pails being taken to the water-taps. Beggars go about hiring babies from the parish nurses. Between five and six the keepers of asses bring them to be milked for the sick. At seven it would seem all the world is at the barber's. At ten the girls and lads go to the Tea Gardens, where they eat rolls and butter, and at this time clerks and suchlike persons take their morning ale and dumpling.

I was pleased to see how many persons carry flowers which they have bought from the flower-gardens outside the Town ; this is strange too, as a friend tells me one third of this vast place is almost penniless.

I bought from Isabella Inglish a Specifick Remedy called " The Grand Angelica," or " The True Scots Pull," at the " Unicorn " over against the Watchhouse near the May Pole in the Strand, and found the Pill excellent good after so much eating and drinking, and take some to my friend Roger Cooper, who do suffer greatly from sourness.

To Hampstead by stage 400 feet above the Thames River, and there saw a multitude of people dancing to music and feasting. Here are many Taverns, shops, bowling greens, the Great Room, and a healing spring.

All about London are Wells, Spas and Public Gardens which all the world go to and make merry at little cost. There is Islington Spa, and Bagnigge Wells, which has many grottoes and arbours; one grotto will hold nigh twenty persons. There is an Inn here where I ate some meat and took ale very cheap.

Of these Pleasure Gardens are Lambeth Wells, Bermondsey Spa, Vauxhall, Ranelagh, Marylebone, and many others where can be seen tight-rope performers, fireworks, and many sights not suitable for godly eyes, yet mothers do take their daughters there, but perhaps to admonish them. Even at Hampstead a well-known Highwayman was pointed out to me.

On Sunday I beheld a curious sight, advised to do so by Sir Moreton Trelawne, and that the streets full of barbers curling men's wigs ready for Church. I took a half-pint of Port at a Tavern and went to Saint Mary le Strand, where an excellent sermon by a Bishop. Later some cold meat and wine in Kensington, having driven there and curious to see how Servants of the Gardens are posted there to keep all meanly-dressed

persons, allowing only well-dressed and behaved persons to enter.

How peaceful is my own Home after this riot, yet the Churches full as well as the Coffee Houses and business good. At the same time the number of poor folk and the blind and maimed, the drunken and the bullies very terrible.

May 1.—We are come now to this sweet Month which the Romans did set aside to Flora, Goddess of Fruit and Flowers. Now we must sow and plant and protect.

(Mem. : To see Spalding do nurse my Roses against night frosts, this being a month of treachery and of knavish days together with sudden heats but lovely withal.)

So far I have had no blights, the Month coming in cold, but my borders must be cleared of Spring flowers, and bulbs lifted and dried, especially those rare bulbs got from Mrs. James Egg's Sale, and the beds must be dressed well against summer planting.

Asters, Marigold and Stocks I have caused to be

sown in open ground, and Marguerite Carnations sown in pots against the Autumn.

" Lilies of the Vale be like little white children in green pavilions." This spoke to me by a drunken fellow whom they call Tom Pot here, but Tom will make cowslip balls for the children to toss up, and tells me how the primrose do sit so demure in Nature's green lap, and brought me once twenty glow-worms in a bottle, " for," says he, " you are so much in your garden, you may need Nature's lamp to say your prayers by."

Last night all the air perfumed by sweetbriar and my thoughts speed back to my young days, when I fought Jack Hughes over L.H., of whom he spoke a foul word. Pinked him and let out some of the blood and brandy, and Honour satisfied. The grass wet then and sweetbriar near by, so I do remember my rash youth but with not over many misgivings as some.

May 19.—St. Dunstan's Day : the good man who pulled the Devil by the nose. On this day my Laburnum shows a hint of yellow and will be gay soon, an this good warm weather last. Such days do make me glad, and now comes that bird of Spring the cuckoo to give voice, calling here and there in the lanes and fields. His mate will lay her eggs in all manner of nests, having no architecture of her own and being a merry vagrant.

My gardener doth tell me the country folk say, " Cuckoo Oats and Woodcock Hay make a farmer run away." This to mean if Spring be backward oats cannot be sown until the cuckoo is heard, and if Autumn be so charged with rain that the last hay cannot be carried until comes the time to shoot woodcock, then must a farmer have a bad year. This is true.

May 21.—Comes John Everglade, Thomas Crawley and Sir Walter Marshall to make merry with me, so, after a good dinner, soup, fish, saddle of lamb and woodcocks, we sat in the garden and set to making a Punch of Brandy, Water, Lemon, Sugar and Spice. Sir Walter Marshall, who is lately out of the East, says that Punch is an Indian word, " punj," which means " fire," so we do have five ingredients or as some do say, " Contradictions." Spirits to make it strong, and water to make it weak ; lemon to make it sour, and sugar to make it sweet.

Sir W. did tell me of his Carnations and Pinks of which he has made a great study, collecting his plants from many sources. Of Flakes and Bizarres he hath a plenty. Note : The Flake hath one colour striped through the petals, and the Bizarre two distinct colour-markings. Also he hath many of the Picotee variety, both spotted and with white or yellow grounds edged with red and purple. What are called Selfs, or flowers of one colour, he hath twelve kinds, and Cloves, Fancies, and Jacks, Painted Ladies, and the Indian Pink; so he told us with much talk of disease and moulds, etc. Very informing and I shall make use of all he told me.

> " The birds nor sow nor reap, yet sup and dine,
>   The flowers without clothes live,
>   Yet Solomon was never dressed so fine.
>   Man, still, hath toys or care;
>   He knows he hath a home yet scarce knows where :
>   He says it is so far
>   That he hath quite forgot how to go there."
>   *Writ by Henry Vaughan, who died* 1695.

31*st.*—I would now sum this Month, the sweet of the year, so rich bedecked with butterflies, birds and flowers. The great and small humble bees go from flower to flower; the peacock, tortoise-shell, cabbage and other butterflies abound hovering over my flower borders. They have no fear of man but will settle on him to sun themselves. These be the unpaid for jewels of God, yet will I try to pay for them in my prayer of thanks.

A man may do worse than kneel at his bedside of a night and recall the days of May, and so sweeten himself by the thought that he will rest more easy in his slumber. So may he dream he lies in bracken curled like a Bishop's crosier, and feel the tendrils of wild honeysuckle wind about his hands.

Thursday.—My dog died. To me this morning Mr. J. Dodder, who looks like an owl in an ivy-bush, so awry is his hair and confused are his garments ; but he is a scholar and unmindful of his habits. He is a shy fellow and the boys do laugh at him in the streets, for which I had some whipped, and now it does occur but rarely.

He did wish to see my few Oranges and Lemons which I have but lately grown in a glass house and thriving mighty well.

We held discourse of the growth of these exotics in this country and he did tell me how to distil orange-flower-water, which I have forgot. But he spoke also of the London Gardens and those of rich men, and how the culture of these trees abounded in Charles II his time. He told me also of the old Physic Garden in Chelsea now much improved and with abundance of herbs.

His Grace the Duke of Devonshire hath the Arlington Gardens small but well kept, and the Kitchen Garden very fine, and many walks curiously kept and elegantly contrived. Here are six of the greatest earthenware pots ever seen, being over two foot within the edge and with holy-oke planted in them.

The greenhouse is very well, but all the garden do suffer from the abundance of soot in the air, and a man may pick nothing and keep clean hands.

The Queen Dowager's Garden (of other days) is yet in Hammersmith. It hath a good greenhouse with a high arrected front to the South. The house is well stored with greens of common kinds, but the Queen not being for curious plants these be lacking, but there be plenty of wall trees.

The gardener of that time was Monsieur Hermon van Guine, a man of great skill and industry, who did raise great numbers of orange and lemon trees by inoculation, with mystils, Roman Bayes, and other green cut into pretty shapes.

(Note : The Orange do get its name from the Arab word, Naranj.)

J. Dodder told me also of Sir Thomas Cooke's

Garden, which was at Hackney, where he hath spent the vast sum of three thousand pounds on it, and hath two greenhouses, and a warren of two acres where he placed two coneys and in a few years they did abound in hundreds. There was also a large Fish Pond and other small ponds fed from afar with pipes.

At Lambeth the Archbishop of Canterbury hath a garden mostly of walks and trees, but with a fine Orangery of three rooms heated by a stove in one centre room.

.   .   .   .   .   .

Tobacco.—The Spaniards call this weed the Holy Herb in regard to the Virtues it hath, and a tobacco I have is called the King of Spain's Windsor, and is a sure cure against many evils. Take a little while after a meal, it will aid the Digestion, and a leaf or two being steeped in White Wine over night is a Vomit that never fails in its Operation ; for one who hath to visit a Dead Man it is a good Companion, and if one has been long over books, or has toiled with the pen, it quickeneth a man and dispels those Clouds which overset the Brain. It is good against noxious smells as Pig Sties, and neither Spider nor Flea can abide it. It is excellent against Rheums and will heat and warm the Stomach. The ash is good against a cut wound to stop the bleeding and to purify it. You may tell how much smoke there be in a Pound of Tobacco by weighing the Ashes after, and what wants of a Pound weight cannot be denied to have been smoke.

In England as in Spain men grind it up into a powder or smutchin and snuff it up their noses with a Quill, and even Serving Maids on the Washblock will draw it into their noses and so fall with a fresh Vigour to their work again. A small ball or pill of Tobacco will help a man against thirst, and in Barbary and other parts of Africk a man may ride three days without food or water, yet live by Tobacco. Very curious.

Last week L. Tompson did bring me for a gift a Pipe Stopper curiously wrought out of wood to imitate a greyhound with a hare in his mouth. He hath the fashion of carving many things out of wood and I have two Apple Corers and six Platters carved by him. (Pear wood.)

.   .   .   .   .   .

Sir T. Clutterbuck to call upon me with his new wife, sweetly pretty yet but a girl and he fifty. He presents

her as if man had never before discovered woman ;
his late wife a year dead, and a scold but with a great
fortune. This child as pretty as April, but a fine
scandal, she having been his wife's maid, yet have
innocence writ all over her. So I did kiss her on both
cheeks, and called for wine and cakes to be carried to
the garden house, where we sat, and Sir T. C. would
have her sing, which she did, though confused at first,
and sang two ballad songs. Anon came my black cat,
to my amaze, with six kitten and one she took by the
scruff and did solemnly lay it at my feet and pleaded
with her eyes for attention. Whereat the girl bundled
all the kittens into her lap and the cat sprang there too
and began to lick them all over, and the girl crooned
over them as pretty a sight as one might see in a day's
march.

Took her round my garden and culled a nosegay for
her whiles her good man closed his eyes (and finished
the sherry), and a pretty picture she made standing in
her sprigged silk, asking the name of this and that, and
telling me how she did wash her face in buttermilk, and
begging a stick or two of orange-wood to clean her nails
with. A good simple girl, but made me feel old.

So, after, did command a dish of tea, which is held a medicine against all disorders, and will prevent drowsiness, for it will quicken the spirits, but Sir T. C. and I take brandy to it, for to my idea it is a bitter dull drink whatever the Physicians may say, and I prefer a good cup of chocolate.

To see the pretty creature sip her tea and eat her cakes in my garden did give me a bout of Melancholy. I fell to thinking my house and garden did need a woman and a child, so I rose saying I would give some orders, that they must stay to dine with me, and would take no refusal, and so went away and walked in my Nut Grove, which is set about the sunken garden, a very privy place with a stone basin of water and great silence.

Many women would wed me for my money and my position, but always would there be the memory of Virginia with me. To-day Lady Clutterbuck hath moved me to these thoughts, for, as she passed by the portrait in my study when I took them after dinner, she stood awhile, looked at me and asked me a question with her eyes, and I bowed my head. Set against the portrait is always a vase full of my choicest flowers, and she asked me, but without speaking, did she care for them, and I answered, " They are all grown for her." Whereat she did take one of the roses from the nosegay I had culled for her and laid it by the vase gently. So I did say, " Dead," and mourned again in my heart, but found in my heart something sweet laid against the bitter and was strangely comforted. Death had lost his sting and the Grave its Victory.

How many times can a man break his heart, set his mind in the strange disorder of Melancholy, lose faith in God and Man because of a woman; curse Life, forswear all contact with the gentler sex, and yet recover in the nick of Time because a child bring him tears to be comforted away ? It is the little things that make one great. A mountain makes a man a mouse : conquer the mountain and all men are mice but yourself.

(Mem. : It do take 5,000 bees to weigh one pound.)

" Of season'd Elm, where Studs of Brass appear,
  To speak of Giver's Name; the Month, the Year,
  The Hook of polished Steel, the Handle turned,
  And richly by the Graver's skill adorned."—*Philips.*

THUS does Philips write of the Shepherd's Crook, and it is a great thought that Bishops carry this as a sign that they be Shepherds of the Flock to watch over them by day and night, for Shepherds did so the Star which showed the Coming of our Lord.

My Shepherd is a man seemingly apart from his fellows, a very religious man, by name Peach, living alone in a small cottage with a daughter whom they do say is not rightly come by and has no friends but old Mother Bidwell, a spinster. (Let him cast the first stone.)

To-day he comes to me for his wages and I gave him an old cloak of frieze for which he is mighty thankful and, indeed, with tears in his eyes, which are blue like to sailors' eyes.

(Note : Sheep-rot is common for Butterwort, Pinguicola Vulgaris, and also for Penny Royal, which are marsh plants, as are also Flukewort and Sheep's Bane, and when they do grow and sheep after them, so will they get foot-rot.)

So I set down my poor Notes of Sheep after Peach is gone.

The Sire is called a Ram or a Tup, and the Ewe is the Dam. Peach did tell me that his grandfather's brother-in-law was a Dartmoor Shepherd, and that of the May 1st morning a Ram is run down to the Ploy Field at Holne and there killed and roasted whole with its skin and fur, and at mid-day all the people run to the roasting with knives and cut off a slice to bring them luck, and they say this is come from the old worship of Baal. In this county we do give a Ram for the prize in our wrestling-matches.

A Lamb he will call lamb until it be weaned and then be will call it a Hogget. A tup-lamb is a tup-hogget, and the ewe a ewe-hogget. If the tup be altered he is a wether-hogget.

After the first shearing then is the tup-hogget called a shearling, and the ewe-hogget a grimmer, and the wether-hogget is called a Dinmont. (So they call a kind of dog a Dandy Dinmont.)

When they shear a second time, then is the shearling called a two-shear tup, the grimmer an ewe, and the dinmont a wether.

On the third time of shearing, the ewe is called a Twinter-ewe, and when she will breed no more, a draft ewe.

Peach is full of old shepherd lore and will say, " A rainbow in the morning is a shepherd's warning, but a rainbow at night is a shepherd's delight."

For rain he says, " Crickets will sing sharply, and swallows fly low." Also that toads will walk out across the road, and frogs will change from green to brown. Sheep will keep away from high land, and when I did ask him what they did here when we have no high land, he told me they will get by trees and all close together. Also the Scarlet Pimpernel will close her eyes, and down fly from the dandelion.

64

He told me a shepherd would liefer see his wife dead than it should shine clear of a Candlemas Day. Moles heave before coming rain, and a cat will clean her whiskers.

These are good things for a gardener to learn, so I put them down, such as " Rain before seven, fine by eleven " or " Between twelve and two you may judge what the day will do."

If a shepherd have no weathercock he will read the wind by the smoke of a chimney or the way leaves turn on the trees.

While Peach talks with me, his dog do lie close at hand, listening to every word, and will tap with his tail to make applause. She is grey, small, old-fashioned sheep-dog and wonderful with sheep. " Yes, sir," says Peach to me, " that dog knows every sheep and all their ailments, and he will bring the one having the greatest sickness before the rest."

The old custom, made law by Parliament in the year of the Great Fire of London, of bringing in wool do still survive. It was made to give encouragement to the business of wool manufacture as against the importing of linen, so I did ask Peach if he would be buried in a shroud of wool, to which he gave me answer that he would, and with a penny sewed into linen over each eye, like to his father and mother and those before them. So I did ask him why, and the simple fellow did make answer that none may know the weather of Heaven, but that it must surely not be hot, as in Hell, so might a man take precaution to go warmly clad, in case of accidents. And he said he had noticed in the church windows that the Apostles were always well clad in thick gowns against the cold. So I gave him a shilling and bade him go eat in the kitchen and take a mug or two of the strong ale I have caused to be made. With that he called upon God to bless me, and went his way.

He is a good man, and a good man's blessing is a fine thing to come by.

.   .   .   .   .   .

June.—I must see that my Herbs be gathered now, though some do not so do, but I had it of D. Thorne to do so now, so that they will retain their virtue and smell sweet, and better dried in shade than sun. Now, also, I have caused my Aromatics to be dried, and have planted Lettuce, etc., to have young and tender salleting.

66

Gather snails after rain and put soot where they do most abound. Set tempting baits for Insects, and look closely at Bees for casts and Swarms.

I have now many Antirrhinums in my borders and very gay, also Iris (divers) and Martagon both Red and White, with Pansies, Sultans, Veronica, Violas, and especially my Carnations of which I am justly proud, so I pluck a good posy and carry it myself to Mrs. H. B., partly to please her, she being a good friend and her husband also, and partly by way of a boast to show how my flowers do flourish. I took also a dish of Roman Nectarines, not one eaten by Wasps because I set Glasses of Beer or Honey by to tempt them from the fruit.

To me comes running Lavinia, Mrs. H. B.'s little maid, and like a flower herself, and calls with sweet pleasure to her mother that Mr. Anderson hath brought his garden with him. So I do come through the house into the Garden, where her mother was, and made fun of it that she must kiss me for my gift, at which H. B. burst out laughing, saying he believed I grew my flowers to get kisses and all very merry. So a bottle of Madeira opened and set out in the Bower, and the

little maid must sip at my glass and then speak a piece
to me writ by G. Herbert :

> " When God at first made man,
> Having a glass of blessings standing by,
> Let us, said He, pour on him all we can !
>
> When almost all was out, God made a stay
> Perceiving that, alone of all His treasures,
> Rest at the bottom lay.
>
> Should I, said He, bestow this on My creature,
> He would adore My gifts instead of Me,
> And rest in Nature, not the God of Nature.
>
> Let him be rich and weary, that at least,
> If goodness lead him not, yet weariness
> May toss him to My breast."

Monday.—Comes Mr. Upton, lately from Bath where he took the waters, and tells me he hath had both liver and purse purged out of him. He says he was yellow as a guinea when he went there and now is white and new-minted like the one shilling left in his purse, for, he says, they bled his gold as they did him.

He writ for me from memory out of a broadsheet printed there :

> " Paid bells and musicians,
>   Drugs, nurse and physicians,
>   Balls, raffles, subscriptions and chairs;
>   Wigs, gowns, skins and trimming,
>   Good books for the women,
>   Plays, concerts, tea, negus and prayers.

Paid the following schemes
Of all who, it seems,
Make charity business their care :
A gambler decayed,
And a prudish old maid
By gaiety brought to despair.

Farewell then, ye streams,
Ye poetical themes !
Sweet fountains for curing the spleen !
I am grieved to the heart
Without cash to depart,
And quit this adorable scene."

Mr. Upton took his wife and two daughters with him to take the waters, and, so he says, for the expense he was put to he would fain believe they took *all* the waters. But he does not complain beyond the manner all men complain who take their wives and daughters away with them to a haunt of fashion. Indeed, his complaint is as fashionable as his gout, he being a warm man who hath great business affairs and well blessed with the goods of this world.

Gave Mr. Upton to eat a thing he had never before seen, and an invention of my friend Mrs. S—— L ——. A feast of wild strawberries served in their pots on the table.

. . . . . .

Though it is a joy to any man who cares for his garden, yet it should be that the cook should take a pride in the Herb Garden.

In mine I have placed many herbs recently which I had not before, as Sweet Cicely, which is Myrrhus odorata, well loved of bees, and my maids do crush the seeds to make oil whereby they may polish the chairs and tables and make them to smell sweet.

I have planted Alecost, or Costmary, also, for to flavour my beer in the brewing, as L. Ripley told me.

But now I must set down of my Lavendars both great and small of which I have a long hedge very charming and a true dainty in the garden.

Men do say it came here first with Southernwood when Queen Elizabeth sat on the throne, and Gerade do mention how it did grow in great plenty in later years in His Majestie's private garden in White-Hall.

Some call it Spike and placed among linen will serve to sweeten it and keep away some disorders.

With my Lavender is Rosemary, or, as the French say, Rose Marine, the plant of the sea-spray, but it be the Virgin's flower of blue, and so it is the Rose of Mary. This must all brides carry in their posies, and it should be planted on a Good Friday, so country folk say, but why that should be used for weddings I know not. Mr. Shakespeare doth say in the play of *Romeo and Juliet* : " Doth not rosemary and Romeo both begin with one letter ? " and Ophelia says, " There's Rosemary—that's for remembrance." But some say it is Venus' flower, being sprung from the sea, and so is useful to lovers. Lord ! when a man speaks of flowers and their history, it seems he must always out-garland them.

SOME GOOD HERBS AND MEDICINAL PLANTS.

Agrimony, for the liver and kidneys.

Balm, against fevers.

Blackberry, to take for dysentery.

Black Currants, excellent good for a tonic.

Bladderwrack. (A woman here cured of obesity by it, after many years, and now J. Pickfield uses it and is reduced after 8 days only.)

Bugle, to be used for harmorrhages.

Wild Carrot, for gravel and dropsy.

Catnep. Do give a man to sweat and so good against colds.

Comfrey. To use, make a poultice to place over ulcers and will cure them.

Eyebright. For weak eyes.

Fumitory, for skin affections caused by stomach or liver.

Heartsease. Some say this is good against epilepsy.

Lobelia. For croup.

Loosestrife, to stop excessive bleeding of the nose.

Mistletoe, they say, is good against St. Vitus' Dance.

Stinging Nettle. About here the people make a beer of this.

Penny Royal. A good thing against wind or sickness.

Plantain. The new leaves good against insect-bites.

Scullcap. To give to nervous persons.

Sorrel. To expel worms from children.

Vervain. In fevers.

Winter Green. Rheumatism.

Wound wort, for bleeding wounds.

The roots of Queen's Delight make a blood-purifier and those of King Solomon's Seal an excellent poultice for bruises.

Some day these old remedies be but an Old Wives' Tale, but they are much used in the country, as are pillows stuffed with poppy-seeds to induce sleep. And many maids make a mash of herbs in hot milk to clear their complexions. So God provides, if Man will but believe.

In my garden I grow Chives, and hold no salad good without a few in it, and to make a Cup what is it without Borage ?

Mem. : To dress a Pike. Stuff it with pickled oysters, winter savoury, thyme and marjoram, and a Trout too is good dressed with herbs. Moths will scorn to come at clothes to do their horrid evil if bitter wormwood be placed with them, and some use Fennel in broths and baked fruits, but I will have none of it.

True it is that even the plants do quarrel, for Rue and Basil will not grow together, nor mint and parsley, nor radish and hyssop. Mint must be in a moist place and Horehound a dry. Elecampane lives in shade and wet, and Saffron sand and sun. As for Vipers Bugloss, it will grow anywhere. The hardy blue fellow like the eyes of Shepherds and Sailors, who are much akin, knowing the stars and reading the weather, as they say, from crown to spur.

．　　．　　．　　．　　．　　．

How many thoughts do come to a man in the cool of the evening ! Thoughts of the great Puzzle of Life and Death and how a man is at last put away in a box of wood under the Earth and none the wiser where he may be but that he be somewhere nigh all men believe. Some have fright of the Unknown, but does any man know what the next hour will bring forth ? This evening found my cat Charles dead in a shrubbery, and bade the gardener place him in the Orchard, under a tree he loved to climb, with, I fear me, intent on birds. I found a spirit of Melancholy come over me and wondering, if I were found dead in my garden, would some one come and mourn over me and place me, also, under a tree, and place a slab of stone over my poor dust to mark where I lay, and who I had been, and then pass away soon from the minds of men.

I was in a sad case, thinking so, when a warm wind set to whispering over my garden and a nightingale sang not far away. Then all suddenly my flowers did breathe out their scent-song and refreshed me right to my soul, so that I thanked God for all His mercies and went in to take my night-cap and my pipe in great calmness of spirit.

.   .   .   .   .   .

Some men take great delight in showing themselves off as creatures of no merit, dealers in trifles and small affairs ; of such account is my old friend Ned Hallet, who speaks of himself as very small fry, which is but his manner of boasting, but harmless withal.

N. H. will engrave the Lord's Prayer on a shilling, cut the image of a man excellent well out of paper, light a bonfire with a pocket-mirror, and comes but lately to me with a wood model of my house so contrived that birds may build therein, " an'," says he, laughing, " you will be Squire and they will be Choir."

I take a great delight in this simple man and cherish his sayings, of which he hath a many. " Though every Man cannot fill his head with learning, 'tis in anyone's Power to wear a Periwig." " Let him who cannot say a witty thing, at least keep his teeth clean."

" I have not the genius for Mathematics," says he, " but I can arch an Eyebrow; introduce a pretty Oddness in the tucking-up of a Gown ; regulate the Dimensions of a Wig ; narrow the hems of bands, and dispute on the Art of Miniatures."

While we sat in my garden comes a neighbour, Mr. Cherwell, whom many thought a mad and bad fellow, but now is held in great respect. He bought of Lord S. his house, park and farms, cut down many trees and made a plan of land-drainage learnt in Holland. And now from being poor and nigh starving, his Tenants are rich and the county glad to buy eggs, chickens, pigs, etc. from the farms ; and each farmer must show exact accounts and show a profit of so much per centum to the acre, and he will have none who do not work hard and so bring prosperity to the neighbourhood. He hath junketings and Holidays, when his Tenants all dress in blue and every maid must carry a posy, for he hath great love of flowers. On July Twelve there is an Exhibition of Flowers, and I am bidden to be the Judge, which do please me most highly. But Lord, the distrust and opposition at first, and he known as Mad George, and an image burned of him on Guy Fawkes Day, but now with me on the Bench with other Justices of the Peace, and Founder of our Society, which we call Gentlemen Gardeners, and the Reports of our Meetings read all over England. N. H. is a Fellow of All Souls, being first educated at St. Paul's School in St. Paul's Churchyard hard against the Cathedral.

(To-day came W. Walter, a great Woollen Dealer, to buy wool from me out of my farms, and before the clip. He hath a shop at the corner of Change Alley in London, which he tells me is 14 foot long and 8 broad, and he must pay 90 pounds a year for it !)

April.—To London again, the snow making the roads very heavy, and causing one of our horses to fall, but to no damage, though an inside passenger, an old woman of a man did cry out we were set upon by highwaymen.

A great flight of rooks and carrion crows over the City in the early morning when they do eat of the filth thrown into the gutters.

Here met me my old friend Bob Fox who would have me stay with him a week to see his collection (very curious) of Roman remains found in London, and has also some flower paintings, newly acquired, by van Heist, or a name akin to that.

First he takes me to his lodging over the Half Moon

79

Tavern out of Piccadilly, where he has all the house but the ground floor, and excellent well arranged that he even have running water to wash in from an old pipe laid by the Romans he tells me and coming to the back door from the Tyburn river.   Very cold.

He carries me to dinner at the Dog & Duck in Carrington Street, where we ate duck stewed in the French manner with onions and potatoes, and a pasty of apple and ginger, and good claret.   Afterwards we sat and watched some young fellows hunting ducks on the pond which is two hundred feet square.

From there to Shepherd's Market, not long built by Edward Shepherd, and here the May Fairs are held, and plays given in the theatre here.

He did also show me, near by, Mr. Deane's school where Mr. Pope, the great poet, was educated.

Near by is Devonshire House, with a fine garden, all built and equipped by Kent.   In the old house, destroyed by fire in 1733, Queen Anne did live when she was but Princess of Denmark.

To refresh ourselves, which my friend did greatly need, he having talked all the while, we entered the well-known tavern up against the Park and called

" The Pillars of Hercules," where is excellent cool ale and good cakes, but stands in a mean place of little drinking houses full of low people. Nearly opposite to this tavern stands one of the old Forts put there in 1642 for the defence of London. So we did cease our peregrinations at the top of Knightsbridge and took coach to our lodgings though they be near by.

The next day R. Fox did read me a paper he is to read before the Society of Antiquarians. It is a paper with much curious matter set down in it of Birds and Cats, so I borrowed it from him to enter pieces of it in my Journal.

For birds of good or evil omen he sets down the Raven, who foretells death if he rest on a house, the Owl will screech for foul weather and sickness, but Swallows and Storks are of good favour. But he says also of the Owl that Minerva, Goddess of Wisdom, chose him for friend, as Juno took the Peacock.

Of the saying, " A little bird told me," he has it that it is out of the Bible, from Eccles. : x. 20. " Curse not the King, no, not in thy thought, for a bird of the air shall carry the voice, and that which hath wings shall tell the matter."

The Turks do say, " It is better to have an egg to-day than a chicken to-morrow."

Of superstitions he do write : " The Chough must not be killed in Cornwall because the soul of King Arthur passed into a Chough."

The Hawk is the form entered into by Horus, the Egyptian god, and their god Thoth escaped from slaughter by disguising himself as an Ibis.

Mother Carey's Chickens, which are Stormy Petrels, are the souls of drowned men, so sailors say.

The Robin plucked a thorn from Our Lord's crown of Thorns, and so had his breast dyed with blood.

The people of Ireland protect the Swan because the daughter of Lir became a Swan and was condemned to wander on Lakes and Rivers until Christianity was brought there.

I have set these down, but he hath collected many others of curiosity to do with the feathered world that he promise me he will send when the paper is in print.

When I questioned him how he came to choose the Bird and Cat for his paper, he told me that the thought came to him of so many lonely old women would have none but them for company, and though they be enemies in the world, yet will a cat learn to leave a cage-bird alone, so three odd creatures, Woman, Cat and Bird, may live in amity.

Mem. : Restoration Jelly for Invalids.

> 1 Pint Port-wine.
> 2 oz. Isinglass.
> 2 oz. Brown Sugar Candy.
> 1 oz. Gum Arabic.

Let these ingredients stand twelve hours.   Simmer on the fire till all be dissolved.   *But do not let it boil.*

Strain through clear India muslin, and pour it out into a dish so as to allow it to be half-an-inch thick, then score it across in squares of about one inch and a half thick when warm.   Several of these to be taken in the day.   (Mrs. McQueen.)

Cassis Cordial.

Peel eight Oranges.
Ditto Lemons.
3 lb. of sugar.
1 Gallon of Gin.

Put the whole into a jar and fasten tightly. Place near the fire, and stir now and again. In ten days strain it through flannel. Bottle, cork and seal it up, and keep as long as you can resist tasting it. (Mrs. Garraway.)

Friday.—Set in to rain, so took to cutting a quill or two and to note what my friend do say of Cats.

R. Fox do note how that the Cat was a symbol of Liberty in that it knows no restraint, and as such was used by the Romans, who made the Statue of Liberty as a woman with a Cat at her feet.

The old Egyptians worshipped the Cat and set it as a symbol of the Moon for that its eyes do wax and wane like the Moon at night, and no man durst kill a Cat under pain of Death.

Mem. : We call a Hare, puss, in my county though no man can say why.

And I remember how Mr. Addison in the Spectator do write of cat-calls in the theatre.

R. Fox is curious also on the Tavern sign The Cat & Fiddle, and says it was from the faithful Governor of Calais, Caton le Fidèle.

The pewters in Inns are still called Cats and

Kittens, and a soldier's little sack is a Kit, as also is a Caldron.

I do find R. Fox to be very jealous in his careful reading and putting down old sayings still used, as " to let a Cat out of a Bag," " All Cats are grey in the Dark," etc. But it is strange to read of Dick Whittington and his Cat, and how he says the story came about. A Cat is a ship very deep waisted and made on the model of those used by the Norwegians, and was used in the trade of coal. D. Whittington, they say, made his money in trading coals from Newcastle.

Mem.: I seem to remember reading in the Cookery Book by Mrs. Glasse, which is the pen-name of Doctor John Hill (still alive), a note for the cooking of Cats to stew them in the likeness of Hares, but I may be wrong since the book is no longer in my shelves. Alas! How much heartbreaking is there in the lending of a book, and how much joy you can give to your friends by so doing so it be one way good. But where do the odd volumes go to? I have my shelves with sore gaps left in them as it were literary teeth torn out and never to be replaced. At the moment I have lost my Bee Book, having entered nothing therein for some

months. I know, as one says, I put it in a safe place,
and so secure is it that none can find it though I caused
my house to be turned upside down. But in this were
many revelations, pieces of good lace found behind
drawers ; an old carved apple cover ; and a multitude
of keys to open the Lord knows what, but they conjure
up no Ghosts as do some things found, but no indiscreet
notes left, for which I am mighty thankful, though, in
my youth, I gazed at the moon as long and ardently
as any boy, thinking to get some answer from her to
ease my delicious pain. A farmer's daughter once
seemed to me the very spit of all the Goddesses, so warm
and comfortable was she and smelt of milk and sweetbriar, but was a good girl and did me no harm, yet
when I pass a cut hayfield in the evening I think of her.
And I should pass her by in the Market now and not
recognise her nor she me, which is perhaps as well.

Memory is the mother of dead children. Bitter
and sweet taste alike after many years, and, though a
young man fail of his promise, he can yet look back to
the days when he breasted the high seas of adventure
and was not afraid.

I set this down here in the silent watches of the night

when this study of mine is full of ghosts who do crowd about me but not unfriendly, and soon the dawn will come with fresh promise. Though the hair upon my face will show grey, and the morning light prove me ashen with weariness, yet shall the sight, smell, sound of my garden refresh me.

Lord, quicken Thou my spirit. Amen.

In a hayfield.—To lie easy in a field of a fine morning
is often the finest physick a man can take. There are
a thousand delights to take the eye, and much diversion
in the goings and comings of the insects. What a
grand carpet hath the good God spread for our delight,
pricked with countless flowers, a home or resting place
for birds, a playground for conies, and the shadowland
of clouds.

Here is the yellow Centaury which do belong to the
Gentian family, as do the Felwort and the Buckbean.
They do best grow in chalk or clay, and there is chalk
here I know. By the edge of the stream which runs
by one side of this pasture is the blue Mouse-ear

scorpion grass, but country folk call it Forget-me-not, and it is a pretty name and good for this pleasant flower. It is because it hath the upper part of the leaf shaped in the fashion of mouse's ear that men named it Myosotis, a Greek word. The Hound's Tongue hath a Greek name also, from Kuon, a dog, and glossa, a tongue, the lower leaves looking like a dog's tongue.

In the ground by me is a dainty thing and smells sweet with the sun on it, but if you pluck it you will see it hath no wish to be culled, for it will roll up its pretty pink cup at once. And this is the Bindweed, which will fold up in wet weather, and at night also, the better to preserve its honey.

There is a plant, though not in this field, that hath an Act of Parliament to itself made in the reign of Queen Elizabeth and is called Marram, but by herbalists by its Greek name Ammonphila, meaning a sand-lover, and the Act was to prevent persons from pulling it up because it will hold sand together as in a net and prevent it from blowing away, thus assisting the firmness of shores. (This I read in a book W. Herbert gave me.)

Here, under the hedge, in the shade where the ground

is moist, is Herb Paris, and low flies as the Dung Fly will come to it for it do stink like carrion. Here too is Verbena, but some call it Vervain, which country folk take as a medicine, or to bring good luck, or to keep off fevers. So the old Romans culled it as an altar-plant.

The Yellow Flag is here too, which humble bees do like for its store of honey, but he must push into his head to come at it, while the Honey Fly with his long tongue can come at it the more readily.

I cannot say the Belladonna grows in this field, but as I passed some the other day I will set down a curious thing not well known. Out of this plant the Italians make Drops to place in the eye so it shall sparkle and the name is come from this, Bella Donna, Beautiful Lady.

Note. (In wild flowers the name " dog," " horse " and " hog " are set against them when they are coarse which is a strange thing.)

In a field.—There be also Codbine and Cream growing by the water, and that is the Willow Herb, a sweet purple flower, and shows well against a dark background or with rushes. I can see Marjoram, which means " hill of brightness " in the Greek, and is a pretty enough purple flower but not yet in bloom. Near by the Marjoram is Water Pepper, which is called also Knot Grass.

There is a plant in this field the name of which I did not know, but seeing two children pass by I did call them to come to me and did ask them how they called it. The boy said at once that his father called it Archangel, but the girl said her mother said it was Weasel Snout, and this did puzzle me, so I made a search in my book and one said it was called Archangel by the monks, who made an ointment from it, and Weasel Snout was given to put it to shame in later years.

My birthday.—To-day do I thank God that He has brought me to my forty-eighth year in fair health, a goodly heritage and money enough in my Bank.

I do find in my study two dishes, one of May Cherries, and one of Strawberries, very artfully set out with their natural leaves, and also a fair vase of flowers, Roses, Pinks, Iris, Asphodel, Jacynth etc. : Also a painting of a Bee the size of nature, and so true one might think it would fly away at any minute ; done by the hand of my dear friend Lady Harriet Forester Dean, which I take to be a marvel, she being nigh sixty and can move but little from her chair in comfort owing to corpulence.

Then did the maids arrive to give me a greeting and

a bunch of flowers (wild) and I was near to tears at the sweet thought of the faithful creatures and bade my man to open four bottles of Port that they might drink my health, and gave each two shillings.

In the garden the sparrows are twittering and a whitethroat has built a nest, and butterflies like flower-petals flit to and fro upon their business. Not even the yew suggests death, nor does a skeleton leaf suggest the grave.

Life is too urgent for young people to notice these things, but sometimes the heart of Youth quickens to see the hedges decking themselves, and a carter's boy will chew the stem of a piece of dodder-grass between his teeth.

I did sit for a while in a gazebo I have caused to be made in the far corner of my South wall. It is made from those oak planks I bought when they pulled down Birdew's cottage to enlarge the Cattle Market. I can come to it by an easy stairway, and have a table and two chairs there, and a jar of tobacco. From this snuggery I like to view the people coming to Market, some driving, some riding, some on foot, and I find it in my heart to pity the poor fowls, geese and ducks slung by the feet head downwards, their necks all turned up to get air into their lungs : they look like living candelabra.

Anon comes a woman sitting astride on the backside of her donkey, with panniers of vegetables in front of her. She trusts to her ass to know his path, and sits, eyes bent on knitting, a kerchief over her head, deaf to all the discord about her.

What a discord it is ! Loudest of all are the pigs who squeal and grunt as if the butcher's knife were already at their throats. Now come the lowing cattle smelling sweet of milk, and now a bull gets loose and charges the scattering crowd, upsetting booths and sending men, women, children, pigs, sheep and fowls in all directions. For a moment he stands King of the Market, with a gaudy piece of cotton caught over one of his horns ; then a young fellow grinning and sweating seizes the pole and ring and holds him.

An old dame tumbled into her store of crocks is helped up with much good-humoured laughter ; sheep-dogs sort out their nervous flocks ; pigs are beaten into their pens ; and a great glossy mare neighs to her colt to bid him be cool and orderly in all the pandemonium.

(These notes I set down as swift as my hand would let me, but Lord I did laugh and mop my eyes, for though this go on week by week it is ever new to me.)

By me, under mine eyes, sets up one of those men common to all our countryside, a travelling herbalist, and to see the country folk scratch their heads and fumble for pennies to purchase some Quack nostrum, is a sight for sore eyes. They do profess to great travel and knowledge of High Quarters in Burgundy and other Courts.

" Look at my herbs," he cries to the gaping crowd ; " they are as good for the poor as for the rich, and I make pennyworths of them, for a man may well have a penny in his pocket who has not five pounds. No ox, nor horse, be he ever so strong, dare eat of these herbs, they are so strong and bitter, yet with my preparation you can eat them. Soak them for three days in white wine, and if you have not white, use red, or if you have neither red nor white, use water, for many a man has a well at his door who has not a cask of wine.

" If you were to ask me if my father and mother were in danger of death, what would I give them, I

95

would give them this. To-day I have only a few packets left; if you want them buy them, if you don't want any, let them alone."

Across the road Nat Arrow hath set his barber's chair on the cobbles and sets about scraping the faces of the farmers, while his boy scours their wigs. Meanwhile their wives are about in the market, cheapening pots and pans, and will wait later by the door of some Inn where they serve a Market Ordinary until their good man come for them. The farmers do go mostly to the White Hart, the cattle and sheep buyers to the Half Moon in Water Lane, the Fen folk who sell birds and game, eggs and butter to the Hole in the Wall, while stewards, horse dealers and corn merchants use the big upper room of the Red Lion. The poorer folk bring their own food and roast slices of meat at braziers, and drink gin out of stone bottles, and by three o'clock most are market-merry and suffer their wives to take the reins when they do drive home.

. . . . . .

To-day, sat at a Drainage Meeting upon divers points, but in particular over the old question of the wooden bridge over the River in the Parish of Snaithe.

This bridge, the maintenance of which hath caused much foul language, is held at the costs of the Lords of the Soil on either bank, and they do take toll of 1*d.* at each end where is a little Toll House of wood. This Toll is held by a Roll of Parliament of Henry VI, 1442. And whereas, on the left bank, the soil hath been held since that date by the Cleethorpes and by them the half of the bridge hath been well timbered and maintained, the part on the right bank hath been held by divers persons but notably by a miser these sixty years and is in ill state for all he doth collect his pennies himself and so save a Toll-keeper. So we do agree the full charges of maintenance for twenty years be held to be his and the whole bridge to be repaired out of these charges. But Mr. Sacktown of Comefleet do pull a wry face and do ask who it shall be who is to pick a miser's pocket, whether a brave and resolute man by force, or a cunning man by argument. So, with much merriment, we did choose him as being both, at which he was mighty displeased.

(Note : added after. Mr. Sacktown did prevail by purchasing the whole Toll Rights and did raise the Toll to 2*d.* to reimburse himself, and did so widen and strengthen the bridge that cattle can now pass over at 1*d*. for two beasts, or six pigs and a light cart 2*d*. : which is now much used since it do save a matter of four miles six furlongs between Barton St. Giles and The World's End Inn.)

After the Meeting we sat down fourteen to dinner provided out of our funds, where a new Punch Bowl of silver was presented by our oldest member, William Hartcross of The Hundred of Leymarsh, and I knowing of this caused it to be filled with roses out of my garden. In my speech I did say that the company would look upon the bowl as of great beauty and a gift much appreciated by all, but that I did spy all eyes looking at the flowers to wonder if they were all the merriment this bowl should hold. So, to cheer their hearts, I rapped on the table with the mallet, and comes in Forster, our serving-man, with a ladle (my gift) and wine and spirits, lemon, ginger, etc. for the making of a Port Wine Punch to the satisfaction of all. Then, to our amazement, did Mr. Sacktown knock on the table, and his man brings in glasses, one for each, with their names engraved on them very pretty. So we did vote him to the Chair and to mix the brew.

After J. G. Ardent told us of a boy hung yesterday for the cutting down of a cherry tree, and this like to be the last case because of public outcry, and none know whence this law came unless it be Roman, they being people who cherished that fruit greatly, or by some Act of Henry VIII to protect his orchards at Sittingbourne.

(Mem. : Lily White Vinegar, 3*d.* a quart bought of the Landlord.)

Note : To use raw turnip to clean dish-covers. Also M. Flitting told me how she makes Brawn, and hers being excellent I shall tell my cook to do likewise.

A Pig's heart, 4 feet and 2 flanks. And 2 Calf's feet boiled until they be quite tender—take out every bone while it is hot. Put it into a form and put weights on it so it may be pressed very hard ; the two flanks to be placed round as an enclosure to the tongue, feet, etc.

June 5th.—To-day is held to be the day of Saint Boniface, that man of Devon who was made Primate of Germany in A.D. 755. This I know because there is a figure of him in Crawfleet Church and in none other for miles. Here we have many churches dedicated to Saint Nicholas, patron of sailors.

On my farms the shearing is in full swing, and next week I must give the Shearing Supper as I always do ; cold meats, pasties, beer and gin, and cordials for the lads. My head man hath clipped 74 sheep without pyking one, which is a great performance, so he shall have a bottle of Port wine and five shillings. I to cut the cake and sing a song, as is my wont and was my father's, after that I leave them to their coarse songs and talk, but they are good men and have stout hearts to their labour.

This year they do tell me the haymaking will be early being a hot season after wet, and the hay not likely to sweat and rage internally when it is stoocked. Some persons cannot come by hay without their eyes and noses vomit water to their great distress, and many men snuff up salt and water to stay this but without much avail.

To see to my rods and have wasps' nests taken so they become not a plague, and also to get the grubs for my fishing, there being plenty of perch, rudd, etc. in the Drains.

My strawberries now ripe and the better for being layered into casks pierced with holes from which they sprout and hang down in garlands, a pretty sight, but O the blackbirds and thrushes do often prevail against nets, though I set springes against them of horsehair. Yet the birds are my gardeners against the pest of insects, grubs, caterpillars, and all manner of small things, so I do balance a pecked strawberry against small slugs.

Now the Water Violet is found by the streams, and the Foxglove shows her purple finger stalls. (Folks Glove.) The willow shines silver, and the birch trees give their elegant dance to the winds.

June 6th.—In the lane at the foot of my garden is a

dog-rose now in bloom and very sweet to smell, so I suffer it to grow over my wall and take pleasure to walk by there in the evening.

My bees come staggering home from the clover and are like to swarm soon. In the garden they cluster about the broom I planted two years ago, and many insects hang about the honeysuckle as if it were a Tavern.

It is the sweet stillness of the long light evenings which do hold me most, being as much like to prayer as may be, though Lord knows I am a sinful man enough yet soothed by garden peace which, of itself, is good. The swifts cease their joyous screaming as the dusk falls, yet one or two will still fly high, then skim the earth as if they looked for lost playmates.

The bats come out like little black ghosts, and the air holds the scents the hot sun brought forth. White roses prick light against dark leaves, and one of my cats moves stealthy across the lawn where the eyes of daisies shine (cut grass to-morrow).

Indoors the maid hath lit my candles in my study, leaving the windows open, the evening being so still and warm. The lights of them through a tracery across the bed of flowers and over the path to the lawn.

My clocks chime the hour yet the world do seem so still that no time seems to pass, and the deepening shadows make my moon dial. A traveller returning late rides past over the stones. So still the night is that I hear the deeper echo as he rides into the Inn yard of The White Horse under the archway.

Men say Night is evil, but they be evil men who say so. Even poor jail-birds are asleep. Soon will the moon come to paint all in silver, blue and purple, and my lawn shall show like a pool with the black tracery of my big acacia tree thrown upon the surface. Then shall I retire to my study, mix my toddy and go to bed at peace with all mankind.

Friday.—Comes a strange man to read a paper to our Society, a Welshman but lately out of that part of France they call Brittany. He did read to us of the Fires of St. John which are lit on every hill-side on the day of St. John and the peasants dance all night round the fires as did people in the days of the Druids. If a maid do dance all night round the fires she is sure to be wed within the year. They do keep a brand from the fire and place it by a piece of box which has been blessed on Palm Sunday by the priest, and with these a piece of Twelfth Night Cake, which three, they hold, will preserve the house from evil by thunder. They place nosegays on the pile before it burned and these will preserve against powerful bodily evils.

Here too, said this gentleman, are great bouts of wrestling held having the same rules as our own in Devon, Cornwall, Cumberland and Westmorland, very strange, yet men say that England and Brittany were once but a short distance across the seas, but he do find no trace of the language in Devon but in Cornwall and Wales only. There are great stones set up by the Druids and even to-day they do hang out a bush of mistletoe over Inn doors.

These people do hold France to be a foreign country and they keep to their own language and dress, their poetry, which is mostly ballads and very sad, and even their fairies have different names, so do they mix fairy, priest and Druid in a manner peculiar to themselves.

Here, in Brittany, they do use for the " asking in marriage " which is done by a tailor, a rod of flowering broom to show he be in office as the " messenger of marriage," and when he do arrive at the house he will lay his rod upon the threshold of the house and cry a blessing upon it in the name of the Father, the Son, and the Holy Ghost. When the marriage has been accomplished then do all repair to the feast, and the rooms are hung with white linen and garlands, the whole very pretty and not a little like to our Harvest Homes, May Days, and the wedding of a farmer's daughter.

Then he read of the feast what do go with the laying of a new threshing floor which is very akin to ours. First do come the carts filled with clay and barrels of water, the clay is thrown out and then the water is poured over it, after that with much singing and laughter the men and girls enter on the cart horses which are all decked out with ribbons of all colours and these go round and round to beat the floor into a good paste and until it be trodden firm. The chief man do then make a mark on the floor with a new flail, after which a feast is spread and nosegays hung about the doors of the barn, and much merriment and dancing together with drinking and old songs, and it being a sight I have often seen albeit that the Breton do wear his coloured vest and loose knee breeches, and we do wear smocks and grey or blue stockings, and here is a violin played while with them it be bagpipes. All these things of ancient times do please me mighty well and I do give a sum of money for the horse best groomed and decorated, and a sum also to the merry making. One year when I was at the dance comes as pretty a wench as you might see but mighty confused, and all the dancing did cease and the floor cleared. Then she do tell me as a forfeit she must kiss me whereat I did make no bones about it but gave her a good round dozen and cry out I am ready for any such forfeits and the more the merrier. Then I did give out that men and girls must all be blindfolded having with me a store of cotton kerchiefs, all blue, and blindfolded them all myself; the men to kiss whom they caught. And I set girls at one end of the barn and men at the other and bade them start. Lord! the fun and laughter but most when S. Waller did catch his own wife and buss her right heartily which they say he hath not done these nine years.

But they have not Plough Monday, which is the first Monday after Twelfth Day, when the men do draw a plough all decorated from door to door of the Parish and ask for Plough money to make a feast. The Queen of the feast is called Bessy though her name be Anne or Kate or whatnot. This feast be for the men mostly and St. Distaff Day be for the women which is on

Jan. 7, when spinning begins. And it was held, and may be yet in some parts that no young woman be fit for a wife until she hath spun herself body, table, and bed linen. So it be that an unmarried woman is called a spinster, and their armorial bearings are painted on a spindle, or lozenge, and not on a shield like to a man's.

Near by to my first farm was an Inn with the sign The Plough and Distaff and there are many such in the country ; but of all Inn signs about here was The Tumble-down-Dick so called for a jest against Richard Cromwell, the son of Oliver Cromwell, and put to show how he was set in high places but to no purpose. But it was burned down and a new Inn built by me and called The Duck and Punt because I do keep my big punt moored there against winter duck shooting.

Writ at The Greenman and Still.—It is strange to light upon a sign such as this but I did come at this place nigh forty miles from my house taking what road I pleased and let my good mare chose her ways. Here, in the heart of the country did she stop before this Inn to take her fill of water at the trough, and there comes an hostler running to me with word of good entertainment to be had there so my belly speaking as well as my heart, for I liked the place well. I cast him the reins and went in to bespeak some dinner. Anon there comes to me a maid as pretty as a blackbird and makes me her curtsey saying how that her father and mother are away to a wedding, so I asked her to whose, and she with a smile and a blush tells me their own which they did forget about come twenty years and she being their child. I did ask her how this did come about at which her blue eyes laughed at me as she tells me that theirs was a parsley wedding and what with one thing and another they had forgot the Church. There did come into my mind then Mr. Shakespeare's Taming of the Shrew where he writes, " I knew a wench married in an afternoon as she went to the garden for parsley to stuff a rabbit."

So I did buss the maid for being so pretty and simple and bade her bring me a draught of ale and set some food before me.

The great chimney beam over the ingle nook had 1551 cut deep in it, and after came an heart with M. F., so when the maid came to set the board I did ask whom M. F. might be, so she told me Mark Farewell and that she was called Merry Farewell and her mother before her was Merry which some said was " old " for Mary.

The ale was strong brewed, with honey in it I think, and the meats good, a fry of pork with onions, a leg, cold, of goose and a dish of plums : after this an hard blue cheese but excellent good.

On either side of the fireplace were set two little

windows scarce six inches square but so placed that a
man can sit and toast himself and look down two roads
(very cunning), for this Inn is placed at the junction
of three roads and hath a triangle of grass before it and
a trough and the sign hanging between two posts.
This sign is after the business of an herbalist for they
do call them " greenmen " in these parts, and the still
is to show he do make cordials. So I called the maid
to me again and asked her if they brewed cordials here
to which she replied that the Farewells had been
" greenmen " for hundreds of years so she had been
told, and she led me to their pot garden which lay
behind the house, and there it lay as neat and tidy as a
piece of patchwork, the still being at the far end and
three skips of bees to the left.

Here were mint and marjoram, liverwort and the
celandine which has a yellow juice and is good for
jaundice. There was herb-dragon also for use against
the bites of serpents, and herb Grace, with herb Trinity
and many others. About this garden was a hedge
with sloes, honeysuckle, foxgloves and wild roses, all
as fine a picture of peace as any man could desire.

Anon there comes a tall lad with half a dozen leather

bottles over his shoulder, and a great stoneware Bellarmine in either hand, and he do call out " Merry " before he sees me, I being partly hidden from him, and the girl comes out and gives him a sound kiss before he puts his jugs down.

Then did I call out and bade them come to me and ordered three pots of beer for us to take. The boy was fair haired with blue eyes and did tell me they were taking up the hay and he was taking more ale to the men at the Squire's expense, so I did place five shillings to it and asked if he could carry that amount of ale with the rest, and they did both laugh at this the lad saying he could carry his ale as well as any man and bade me, with a rustic grace, step up to the field. I did do so and lay me under an old oak in the shade whence I could see men and girls toiling in the field, they being gleaming with sweat in the sunshine and as brown as berries.

There did I lie content and watched the meadow browns and the Venus eye butterflies flitting over the grass until a sweet sleep stole upon me.

For full two hours I did sleep in the shade of the oak and woke much refreshed, and did then watch the last hay wain creak up to the big square rick, then I walked back to the Inn, ordered my horse which the maid did bring, paid my dues and so rode home.

Life is well ordered for some men, they may not read print or make more than their mark with a pen, but they have the stars to read and the Seasons, and make the sun and the flowers their clock by day, and the stars the same by night. They do plough, sow, reap, gathering in harvest and eating of what they have helped to grow, and in the end they go back to the earth laying in God's Acre having earned, please God, a place in heaven. True that there be both men and women who live evil, but in life I do find more good than evil and more kindness than crossness.

June 30.—When a man has engaged to keep a Stage Coach he is obliged, whether he has passengers or not, to set out : so it be with a man who hath engaged in Life, he must set out upon his Day's Travel. This is so beautiful I could well sit and meditate or even ruminate like the beasts of the field and well nigh do so but that my housekeeper comes with the books and I can see my Gardener having the tail of his eye upon me it being the end of the month.

With my housekeeper comes, as ever, a tale of the maids' misdeeds as broke pannikins, loitering with youths, and of how they would eat a man out of house and home. Most of this I know for each month she tells me of this and that and that because a woman must make little worries with which to spice her life. But I must see Moll, she do tell me, to admonish her.

Anon comes Moll, a fine black-headed wench, twisting her apron between finger and thumb.

So I put on my spectacles to feel wise thereby and ask her of her doings with youths in the lanes. Then did she hang her head and told me three lads did court her and how could she help it. I, for my part, could not see how the lads could help it, or she either, for she is a wholesome pretty piece, and June and lanes and Youth are the very Devil; but this I could not say, but warned her as well as I might, (though not easy) and asked if she preferred one particular youth and if so to bring him to me. And I did call to mind how old Mrs. K., who had once been a great toast, told me that in a woman's life there was one to hug, one to marry, and one to regret : so I told her to go about her work and be careful of young men, and choose him who was most sober, honest, and hard working : at which she thanked me so prettily that I was feign to bid her run away quickly to her work.

Mem. : After I had spoke to my Abigail I called to mind that the faithful servant to Queen Anne was Abigail Hill, afterwards Mrs. Masham, so do we get, perhaps, to call our maids Abigails, though the ancient Abigail was wife to King David, the Psalmist.

July 12.—This morning up betimes and rode into the country to visit R. Peachfield whom I had heard lay sick, and as I rode did hear a shepherd boy piping but he did so but so far on an air when he did stop of a sudden before the bar was finished. And I thought so life do break on a song grave or gay and is very rarely brought to the finish of a tune, as a man is killed in battle in the hour of Victory, or a Bride die on her way to Church. Yet the morning was not melancholy but was filled with the song of laughs and the hum of bees. So did I come to R. Peachfield's house to find he has died but an hour before which would be about the time the shepherd boy stopped on a note. But he died blessing his friends and mentioning me by name for which I am thankful for he was a good man.

June 21.—Fine Ladies, young Beaux in Town are just now yawning their ways into their beds after a night of dice and cards, while I am but just out of my bed and sitting by my window to watch the dawn arrive.

Already the morn be warm and an heavy dew do lie upon the lawn, silver-grey yet with dewdrops which the first touch of sun will cause to vanish. Then the pink tips of Apollo's fingers shall break the silver mirror of the sky and all the store of sea pearls in the world look pale before the clouded opal of the new-born day. No soul stirs as yet and even the cock still sleeps upon his dunghill. But one thing moves and that a butterfly as blue as sailors' eyes who sails above the lawn queening the new day.

In Town now how do they greet the day? I set down here the lines of Mr. Humphrey Wagstaff printed in The Tatler of April 30, 1709.

" The Slipshod 'Prentice from his Master's Door,
   Hath par'd the Street, and sprinkled round the Floor.
   Now Moll hath whirled her mop with dext'rous Airs,
   Prepar'd to scrub the Entry and the Stairs.

The Youth with broomy stumps begin to trace
The Kennel Edge, where wheels had worn the place.
The Small-Coal-Man was heard with cadence deep,
Till drown'd in shriller notes of Chimney Sweep.
Duns at his Lordship's Gates begin to meet,
And brick-dust Moll had scream'd through half a street.
The Turnkey now his Flock returning sees,
Duely let out o' nights to steal for Fees.
The watchful Bailiffs take their silent stands,
And Schoolboys lag with satchels in their hands."

I had but writ this when my lord the cock do crow as if he and he alone had caused the sun to rise and disperse the morning mists. Now do my trees and flowers put off the grey month of sleep, and I do hear the rattle of a pail in my stable yard.

Mem. : The cock is dedicated to three heathen Gods, the first, Apollo, because he be herald of the Sun ; the second, Mercury, because he summons men to the work of the day ; the third, Æsculapious, because he calls on men to be early to rise, and early to bed so they be healthy, wealthy, happy and wise. The old Romans did put three of the morning to be cock crow and did call it " gallicinium," I think.

September. In my Bee Book.—Now I must no longer delay to take my Bees, and set to strengthen the entrance to the Hives leaving only a small entry.

There is much to do in the making of Cider and Perry and my Presses are all at work in my Orchard here as well as at my farms.

I do not make much of Perry for it is an oversweet drink I think but ladies like it, but of Cider I make both Sweet and Sour and keep the best for myself and the rest for the men and maids. Now also I must transplant Esculent or Physical Plants, also Asparagus and Artichocks.

Yesterday there did come a Great Wind causing havoc in the fruit trees so, to-day, I have caused the windfalls all to be gathered up and stored separate from the unbruised fruit.

This month I do sow Lettuce, Radish, Spinage,

Skirrets, Onions, Scury-grass and Ani-seeds, also Winter Herbs.

Mem. : To try a dish (told me by Mrs. Harbinger) of Carp roast with a sauce of the Verjuyce Grape which I have growing.

My Bishop Pears, for baking, are now ready, as is also the Lewis Pear which do make an excellent good Conserve, and do dry well for stewing later in the year. Another Pear I have for baking is the Black Worcester but this year something hath come at it and the back must be stripped and treated with turpentine and clay. Later I must lay bare the roots and dress them for this tree is overhasty in blooming.

To-day rode forth to see the body of Bat Malone what is hung in chains by the side of the London Road about six miles from Spalding and set there to be an example to evilly disposed persons who rob wayfarers. He was a low-toby man of great repute and in these foolish times nigh on being accounted a hero.

Mem. : An High-Toby man do rob on the High Road, and a Low-Toby Man on the By-Road.

The people about here give him a gentleman once fallen upon evil times, and from evil times to evil company, so did he become fruit for the gallows tree.

It is a strange thing how men will come to stare at a rotting corpse swinging in chains in its last dance for which the Four Winds do call the tune, yet did I come there myself like any common man to stare but with the lie in my heart that I must needs add a Gallows Tree to my collection. Yet here was once a man who had known a mother, and the joys of childhood, and, as a man told me had been of good family brought up with schooling brought to this pretty pass to be mocked at by birds and men.

I was ashamed but interested, and I could not help but think that this poor thief had a cross to himself but all alone. Yet there was a young girl there full of life on a chestnut horse and she did point with her whip at the body swinging there and laugh as it were at a rarer show, but the youth with her doffed his hat with a fine gesture and sat stern and grim mouthed looking at the corpse. " Come, Tom, what ails you ? " I heard her say. " 'Tis but carrion." And he did reply, " Aye, but 'twas a man once."

I did wonder if the Mandragora or Mandrake would

grow here as old superstition hath it, and that it be a creature having life engendered under the earth of some dead person put to death for murder.

Coaches, chaises, riders went by on the turnpike and every driver and horseman did point his whip. After a while I rode back to Spalding and so into the White Hart Yard.

I was but ill company for myself and did rejoice to see Jerry Clayworth seated in the Coffee Room discussing a pint of sherry all alone.

As Horace says, " Spectatum admissi risum teneatis ? " which is, to put it freely, " Would you not laugh admitted to the sight ? "

Jerry is one with whom a man must laugh. He had the girth of a cart-horse and the heart of a child, and when he cried, " Stap me if it is not old Adam the Gardener ! " I did feel young again and called for the drawer to set more wine before us. In place of the drawer comes a girl at which Jerry must needs cry, " Adam calls, and Eve comes." So did I laugh too and the clouds of my black mood did vanish.

When the wine arrived Jerry do tell me how he is lately from Town where he had business, and was there prevailed upon to see if Mr. Addison were right concerning the Opera. He did tell me he being muchly diverted by a paper on the Opera in the Spectator did see much as was wrote. So he must needs read me out of the sheet of Tues. March 6.

" I must inform my Reader, that I hear there is a Treaty on foot with London and Wife (who will be appointed Gardeners to the Theatre) to furnish the Opera of *Rinaldo and Armida* with an Orange Grove ; and that the next time it is acted the Singing Birds will be Personated by Tom Tits. The Undertakers being resolved to spare neither Pains nor Money for the Gratification of the Audience."

He placed this paper again in his pocket, where, said he, it lived in company with Way Bills, Last Words and Confessions, Recipes for Sheep Dip, A Certain Cure against Marriage, and divers Naughty Papers ; also a sample bag of Corn, a Three pronged Fork in a Case, a Paper of Carraway Seeds and a Purse of Money.

None do know better than I of his way of Half Child and Half Wise Man, he can, indeed, keep a child in roars of laughter and an old dame crying, " For

shame of you, Mister Clayworth, but pray continue,"
as no man can. In Charity he is excellent, and in
Country Lore profound, yet will quote the Holy Bible
against any man and tease a serving Wench about a
Garter in the same breath, and I doubt if he have an
ounce of Evil in him. It do my heart good to see and
hear him. He will kiss the serving Maid, (which he
did and bade me do likewise which I did, he telling
her a good man's kiss be worth all of a bad man's
purse, for the one is full of good meaning and the other
empty of all but another man's money,) and then bade
her bustle about to get a good pie he had seen in the
kitchen served up to us.

I would as lief have this man to lean on in a storm
as many a godly man in the stress of Tempest of either
Mind or Body.

" I shall go to the Grass," said he, " with neither
Headstone nor Tailstone, and if so be you visit my
remains set on the Grass some Hedgerow Flowers and
none of your Trimmed Roses and Lillies out of Polite
Society."

So did I ride home indifferent to wind or weather,
my heart being full of the strange things one may

meet in a day, a rotting corpse, the young and maid, my good friend Jerry, all part and parcel of the tangled story we live when we see and know almost everybody but ourselves. The onlooker, they say, sees most of the game, but in return those in the game see and know nothing of the onlooker.

In life, I feel, I should like a little applause as when a man says " I have never seen you look so well," even that, but I do get it now and again, thank God, but it comes sweetest to me when a child will smile thanks for a gift which is worth nothing.

Afterword.

THE RICH AND ROYAL MAN

I HAVE edited this Diary as well as I could, but it
has not been an easy task in the jangle of traffic which
whirs past my window, nor is it easy to fit the feet
of our modern life into the orderly pattern of the calm
existence of this country gentleman.

To me the reading of these notes has been like
observing the reflections of white clouds in a clear
pool. I have but little sympathy with jazzed hours,
negroid melodies, speed, or restaurant clatter. Now
and again it is good to breast the tide of life, swim
with the strong and battle with raw, naked fact, but
more than ever to-day one needs a backwater, a place
of friends and books, an ordered place, a place
with flowers, where the trumpet-call is not heard, and

the mind has time to ease itself, add up its little learning, arrange its affairs, cast vanities aside.

Actors as we are, we cannot always be upon the stage, and every man must have his reservations, a retiring-place in the wings, a place where he can take off his mask : so I found a kind of ante-room to life in this man's tranquillity, and rejoiced in it.

Out in the hall hang the motley, the cap and bells, the cynic's armour, the megaphone we have to use to-day if we want a hearing. Some of us were killed in the War and still go on living.

Suddenly a voice says, " Courage ! " and you look into the commonplace street and see Youth go by unafraid, clean, vigorous, conquering. That, to be vulgar, makes you pull up your socks and stop squealing about yourself and your little twopenny funk of Life. Sound of wind and limb, you join in the battle, stick a flower in your buttonhole, whistle, and sniff the breeze. By the way, I wonder who the jolly-minded tailor was who first thought to give a resting-place for flowers over your heart. It is a gay thought, and wholesome.

It is a thought which carries me back to my eighteenth-century friend who loved his garden so well.

It makes one know why a jeweller will spend hours and hours making a little mechanical singing-bird not entirely for gain but from a desire to express joy. Away, dull care. Look at that child bowling a hoop along; she flashes a smile to you and your heart goes pitter-pat with delight, as if a little drummer sat there who had only been waiting for the signal to begin.

How wonderful the world would be without money, or if everybody had a modest competence; not all the same amount, that would make life flat, but enough to buy the cheaper luxuries, flowers and song, and an idle day by running water, where you could watch the water-wagtail swagger and a kingfisher flash by like a jewel on wings. " A book of verses underneath the bough,"—that's the idea. To watch water-lily buds bob under and come up again as if a fish had ducked their heads for fun. To see a heron in his leisurely, disdainful flight, to see cows stand orderly at milking-time, and the proud sheep-dog marshalling his flock.

And all out of the sound of the Market Place, away from hucksters, away from barter and jostling crowds.

That is why I like my quiet friend, just as I sometimes long for the smell of hay, or stables, or to press a dandelion-stalk on the back of my hand to make a magic brown circle, or to stand ankle-deep in snow, or wash thought away by swimming in the sea.

Do you know the taste of honey in clover, or the smile of a lake of blue-bells in a wood? Do you know the sweet smell of cows' breath, and the pleasant tangy scent of horses? Do you know the grateful scent thirsty trees give out after rain, the muddy smell of river-banks, and have you walked chewing a cowslip stalk across a field, or lain on a warm bank where wild thyme grew?

If this is hedonism I cannot help it.

Lightning Source UK Ltd.
Milton Keynes UK
UKOW02f1153070515

251064UK00001B/118/P